W9-BNE-206

DISCARDED

DORLING KINDERSLEY DK EYEWITNESS GUIDES

NATURAL DISASTERS

Buddhist statue
survives tsunami

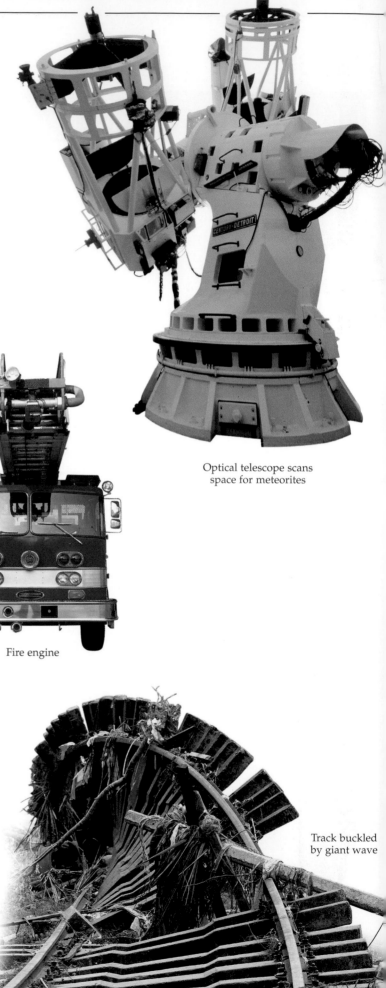

Optical telescope scans
space for meteorites

Fire engine

Doppler
radar dome

Track buckled
by giant wave

DK EYEWITNESS GUIDES

NATURAL DISASTERS

Written by
CLAIRE WATTS

Consultant
TREVOR DAY

Hurricane warning
flags

Spirit of
Smallpox carving

Planet Earth

Seismograph

Body casts,
Pompeii

DK
DK Publishing, Inc.

LONDON, NEW YORK, MUNICH,
MELBOURNE, AND DELHI

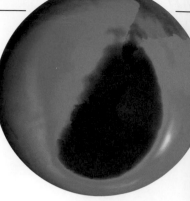

Ozone hole over
Antarctica

Project editors Jackie Fortey
and Carey Scott
Designers Johnny Pau
and Samantha Richiardi
Senior designer Owen Peyton-Jones
Managing editor Camilla Hallinan
Managing art editor Sophia M. Tampakopoulos
Publishing managers Caroline Buckingham
and Andrew Macintyre
Category publisher Laura Buller
Production controller Gordana Simakovic
Picture researchers Celia Dearing,
Julia Harris-Voss and Jo Walton
DK picture library Rose Horridge
DTP designer Andy Hilliard
Jacket designer Sarah Ponder
First American Edition, 2006

Published in the United States by
DK Publishing, Inc., 375 Hudson Street,
New York, NY 10014

06 07 08 09 10   10 9 8 7 6 5 4 3 2 1

A Cataloging-in-Publication record for this book
is available from the Library of Congress.

ISBN-13: 9780756620721 (hardcover)

ISBN-13: 9780756620738 (library binding)

DK books are available at special discounts for bulk purchases
for sales promotions, premiums, fundraising, or educational use.
For details, contact: DK Publishing Special Markets,
375 Hudson Street, New York, NY 10014
or SpecialSales@dk.com

Colour reproduction by Colourscan, Singapore
Printed in China by Toppan Printing Co.
(Shenzhen) Ltd

Discover more at

www.dk.com

Tsunami warning
buoy

Trapped-person
detector

Mayan rain god

Harbor
wave

Smokejumper

Contents

Lava fountains erupt from Mount Etna

Dynamic planet

PLANET EARTH provides us with the air, food, warmth, and materials we need to thrive. But Earth can also generate catastrophic disasters, from tsunamis and landslides to tornadoes and wildfires, that kill people, damage the environment, destroy property, and disrupt normal life. Such disasters may be sudden and violent, like an earthquake or flood, or gradual, like drought or the spread of a deadly disease. Today, scientists have shown that many such disasters are caused by the natural workings of our planet. There are more than 700 natural disasters every year, affecting around one person in 30.

TSUNAMI STRIKES LISBON
This picture of the 1755 earthquake and tsunami that destroyed Portugal's capital, Lisbon, shows buildings leaning at impossible angles. Before today's instant news media, and before photography, facts and images were often exaggerated.

RESTLESS PLANET
The way Earth behaves is controlled by the Sun and by the inner workings of the planet itself. Energy from the Sun drives the weather, and is the source of disasters including extreme events such as droughts, floods, and hurricanes. Heat from within Earth causes movement of the rocks beneath us, which can lead to earthquakes, volcanoes, and tsunamis.

Land heaved upward, leaving this house at a precarious angle

RIVERS OF LAVA
Fiery torrents of lava spew out of Kilauea, in Hawaii. Kilauea is one of the most active volcanoes in the world, erupting almost constantly. There are more than 1,000 active volcanoes on land today, surface signs of the immense pressures and high temperatures deep below ground.

DEVASTATING EARTHQUAKES
Earthquakes are among the most feared of all natural disasters. This street in Ojiya City, northern Japan was turned on its side following a quake in October 2004. During the 20th century, there were almost 1.5 million deaths from earthquakes and, as the world's population grows, earthquake fatalities are likely to increase. In October 2005 a single quake killed 38,000 in Pakistan. Survivors of earthquakes are frequently left with nothing but the clothes on their backs, as buildings collapse and transport links, electricity, water supplies, and telephone links are cut. Essential services such as hospitals may not be able to operate normally. People can lose their livelihoods, too, as farms, factories, and offices are ripped apart.

BLAZING FORESTS

Wildfires such as this one, which struck Big Sur, California, may be ignited by lightning, or by someone dropping a match. They can destroy hundreds of acres of fertile forest, leaving a scarred and seemingly lifeless landscape. However, the damage they cause is only temporary. The forest has the natural ability to gradually regenerate itself. But if the wind blows the fire toward an urban area, buildings and people's lives may be at risk from the oncoming flames and the clouds of choking smoke.

New growth as first rainfall germinates seeds

A DRY WORLD

As the world's population grows, so the demand for water is increasing. Evidence suggests that human activities such as cutting down forests are changing local weather patterns, making droughts more likely. More than 100 million people in over 20 countries in Africa, Central Asia, and South America currently suffer the effects of drought.

DEADLY DISEASES

Most diseases that cause widespread illness and death come from microscopic organisms, such as the malaria-carrying parasite that lives in the saliva of mosquitoes. Forty percent of the world's population lives in areas where there is a high risk of catching malaria. Attempts to eradicate the disease and to create a vaccine have so far been unsuccessful. Malaria continues to kill more than one million people every year.

Piercing mouthparts for drawing blood

Residents carry their possessions as they flee the dangers of the erupting volcano

ESCAPE

In 1984, 73,000 people were evacuated from their homes around the Mayon volcano in the Philippines. Scientists monitoring the volcano's activity had been able to predict a coming eruption. Modern technology, such as satellites that help meteorologists to produce accurate weather forecasts, means that many major disasters can be predicted, giving people time to prepare for the crisis.

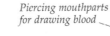

Restless Earth

Diamond embedded
in volcanic rock

DEEP INSIDE EARTH, temperatures and pressures are so great that they can transform carbon deposits into diamond—the hardest of all minerals. Earth's surface, or crust, is divided into massive slabs called tectonic plates. Some of the plates are crunching together, some drifting apart, while others grind past each other. The intense heat and pressure inside Earth disturb the tectonic plates. When released at Earth's surface, the pressure and heat can cause earthquakes, volcanoes, and tsunamis. This can have devastating consequences, particularly for regions close to the edges of the tectonic plates.

South America and Africa fitted together

Atlantic Ocean now separates South America and Africa

PANGAEA
The plates that make up Earth's surface have been moving and changing shape ever since they formed, at least 3.6 billion years ago, bringing continents together and splitting them apart. Around 200 million years ago, at the time of the dinosaurs, all the continents were part of one landmass known as Pangaea.

EARTH TODAY
Over the last 200 million years, the tectonic plates between Europe and the Americas have moved apart, opening up the Atlantic Ocean. Each year, the continents shift by at least 1 cm (nearly half an inch), in some cases, much more than this. In another 200 million years, the map will look different again.

Continental crust

Upper mantle

Lower mantle

Outer core

Inner core

Oceanic crust

EARTH'S LAYERS
Earth's land surface is formed of continental crust, which is typically 45 miles (70 km) thick. The seabed lies on oceanic crust, which is just 5 miles (8 km) thick. The entire crust floats on hot, semiliquid mantle. At the center of the planet is Earth's metal core, which reaches temperatures of 10,800°F (6,000°C).

African plate

Eurasian plate

Pacific plate

Arabian plate

Philippine plate

Indo-Australian plate

TECTONIC PLATES
Earth's crust is divided into about 20 tectonic plates, which fit together like the pieces of a jigsaw puzzle. The plates move very slowly around Earth's surface, powered by the planet's inner heat. Along the edges of the plates, the crust is constantly being destroyed or new crust created. These processes are the cause of most of the world's earthquakes and volcanoes.

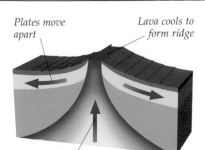

Plates move apart

Lava cools to form ridge

Magma rises from the mantle

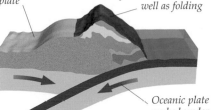

Continental plate

Mountains formed by volcanic action as well as folding

Oceanic plate pushed under

Fault line

Plates slip past each other with a jerk

DIVERGENT BOUNDARY

When plates move apart, or diverge, new crust is formed by molten rock rising into the gap. Along the middle of the Red Sea and its right-hand arm, the Gulf of Aqaba, the African and Arabian plates have been diverging for 50 million years. Most divergent boundaries in oceans form ocean ridges, such as the Mid-Atlantic Ridge.

CONVERGENT BOUNDARY

When an oceanic plate moves toward, or converges with, a continental plate, the oceanic plate is pushed down (subducted) beneath the continental plate, creating a steep-sided trench in the ocean floor. The subducted crust melts into magma, which then rises through the continental crust to form a volcanic mountain range, such as the Andes in South America.

TRANSFORM FAULT

A place where two plates slide past each other, such as the San Andreas fault on the Pacific coast of the US, is called a transform fault. Friction between the rocks may make the plates jam. Gradually, pressure builds up until the plates slip past each other with a violent jerk, causing an earthquake or triggering a tsunami.

NEW CRUST

Wherever magma (molten rock) emerges from Earth's mantle, new crust is created. This may happen in a violent volcanic eruption or, more gently, as the plates diverge. Magma also leaks through weak points in Earth's crust at hot spots far from the plate boundaries. As the plate moves gradually over the hot spot, the magma—called lava once it reaches the surface—may form a chain of volcanic islands, such as the Hawaiian or Galápagos islands.

As lava cools, it hardens into rock

Steam rises as hot lava flows into the sea

What is a tsunami?

THE FIRST SIGN of a tsunami (soo-nah-mee) approaching the coast may be a sudden swell in the ocean, like the surge before a storm at sea. But a tsunami is no storm surge. Tsunamis are caused by massive shifts, or displacements, of water, usually due to movements of the sea floor that accompany undersea earthquakes. They are the deadliest of all waves. They can travel at speeds of 600 mph (950 km/h) and, when they reach the shore, can be as high as 100 ft (30 m). A tsunami may not be just one wave, but a chain of waves, and the first is rarely the biggest. Massive walls of water can slam against the coast for hours, stripping sand away from beaches and tearing up trees and vegetation. The fast-moving water can sweep inland, flooding fields and wreaking havoc on towns and villages.

THE GREAT WAVE
This famous Japanese painting by Katsushika Hokusai shows a towering wave. Tsunamis used to be called tidal waves, but it is now known that they are not caused by tides. Today, they are called by their Japanese name, which means "harbor wave."

LANDSLIDE
Tsunamis can be caused by massive landslides into the sea. As debris plunges into the water, the accompanying splash and sudden displacement of water can generate a violent tsunami. However, tsunamis started by landslides usually affect only the local area and quickly subside.

Soufrière Hills volcano, Monserrat, 1997

Clouds of smoke and ash cascading from Mount Pelée, Martinique

VOLCANIC ERUPTION
When Mount Pelée on the Caribbean island of Martinique erupted on May 7, 1902, the volcano sent out a torrent of volcanic gas, ash, and rock fragments called a pyroclastic flow. When this material fell into the sea, it caused a tsunami that devastated the island's harbor.

IMPACT FROM SPACE
Every day, hundreds of meteorites like this one fall from space. Most burn up in the atmosphere to become shooting stars. Of those that reach the ground, many land in the ocean and simply sink to the bottom. If a huge meteorite—such as an asteroid—hits the ocean, its impact may cause a tsunami.

Meteorite composed of stone and iron

EARTHQUAKE
Most tsunamis are caused by earthquakes around the edges of Earth's tectonic plates. When an earthquake strikes, huge cracks in the ground can open up, as in this salt marsh in Gujarat, India. When this occurs under the ocean, the shock waves from the violent movement can cause a tsunami.

Satellite image of a section of the coastline of Sumatra before the tsunami of December 26, 2004.

AFTER THE TSUNAMI
The worst natural disaster of the early 21st century started when an earthquake measuring 9 on the Richter scale shook the sea floor 150 miles (240 km) from the coast of Sumatra in the Indian Ocean. The tsunami that followed traveled 2,800 miles (4,500 km) in just seven hours, killing more than 200,000 people. When the water receded, the forests, villages, fields, and roads in low-lying areas had been stripped bare and covered with mud. Sand and rock had been swept away from the beaches, changing their shape. The surrounding sea was full of mud and debris.

Mud and debris cover the beaches

Vegetation stripped away, exposing rock and soil

Tsunami grows higher, reaching up to 100 ft (30 m) before it breaks

Decreasing depth causes the waves to slow down

Waves, less than 3 ft (1 m) high, ripple outward from the disturbance. They travel at up to 500 mph (800 km/h)

Giant ripples produced by water displacement

Crack in ocean floor created by earthquake

Direction of fault movement

FROM EARTHQUAKE TO TSUNAMI
When an earthquake causes a sudden shift in the seabed, the displaced water creates a chain of giant ripples moving at great speed away from the disturbance. They can travel vast distances without slowing down. Near the shore, shallow depths force the waves to brake sharply. They slow down and grow higher until they crash onto the shore.

Wave power

Tsunamis caused by earthquakes and volcanoes—tectonic tsunamis—are powerful enough to reshape coastlines and can travel thousands of miles across oceans. Local tsunamis, caused by landslides, can cause higher waves than tectonic tsunamis, but these do not usually travel very far. When earthquakes generate both tectonic and local tsunamis, the effect can be devastating. The biggest tsunamis of all are caused by meteorite impacts. But it is not just the origin of the tsunami that affects its power. If a tsunami invades a bay, the shape of the coastline can channel the waves, making them narrower, higher, and more destructive.

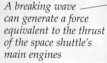

A breaking wave can generate a force equivalent to the thrust of the space shuttle's main engines

HARBOR WAVE
On November 18, 1867, the steamship *La Plata* was struck by a tsunami that hit the island of St. Thomas, in the Virgin Islands. An earthquake measuring 7.5 on the Richter scale had sent a tsunami racing toward the coast. Eyewitnesses described a wall of water 20 ft (6 m) high sweeping over the island's harbor.

Rock face stripped of vegetation by the tsunami is still bare 14 years later

THE BIGGEST TSUNAMI
On July 9, 1958, an earthquake measuring 8.3 sent 100 million tons of rock crashing into Lituya Bay, Alaska. A giant splash surged to a height of 1,720 ft (525 m), stripping away the vegetation to leave bare rock. A rock slide then created a local tsunami over 100 ft (30 m) high—the largest tsunami in recent history. It swept across the bay, flooding inland and uprooting thousands of trees.

SEA SCULPTURE

The extraordinary towers and caves of Cathedral Rocks, New South Wales, Australia, were cut away from the cliffs and gouged out in just a few minutes by the power of a tsunami thousands of years ago. According to scientists, the rocks must have been sculpted by the most powerful types of tsunami—caused by a huge meteorite hitting the ocean or a massive landslide on the seabed.

Oil-carrying truck hurled around by tsunami

BURNING WATERS

On Good Friday in March 1964, an earthquake off the Alaskan coast caused landslides that created a 30-ft (9-m) local tsunami in the town of Seward. Oil-storage tanks along the bay were damaged and their fuel ignited. Twenty minutes later, the first 40-ft (12-m) wave of a tectonic tsunami washed in, spreading a wall of flaming oil into Seward and setting most of the town on fire.

TSUNAMIS AND TIDAL BORES

When a tsunami-generated wave reaches a river mouth or a bay, the shape of the land on either side funnels the wave into a narrow, high wall of seawater weighing billions of tons. Exceptionally high tides create similar walls of water called bores. Here, a tidal bore sweeps over the embankment of the Qiantang River in eastern China, surprising tourists. Bores along the Qiantang River have been as high as 30 ft (9 m), moving at 25 mph (40 km/h).

Walls of water

THE EARTHQUAKE that triggered the Indian Ocean tsunami of December 26, 2004 unleashed energy equivalent to the detonation of thousands of nuclear weapons. Ocean waves radiated out from the undersea earthquake close to the island of Sumatra in Indonesia. The strongest traveled east and west. Bangladesh, to the north of the epicenter, had few casualties, while Somalia, far away to the west on the coast of Africa, was hit much harder. But the pounding waves did not hit only those coasts in a direct line from the epicenter. Some waves were bent around land masses to hit coasts away from the epicenter, such as the western coasts of Sri Lanka and India.

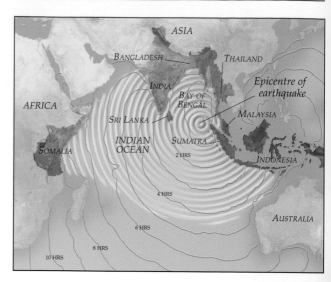

TSUNAMI TRAVEL TIME
Shock waves spread out from the epicenter of the earthquake like the ripples when a stone is dropped into water. Each pink line on the map indicates one hour of travel time. The waves took just 15 minutes to reach the nearest land, Sumatra. Seven hours later, the coast of Somalia was struck. The effects of the tsunami even caused minor damage as far away as northern Australia.

SEISMOGRAM
This seismograph reading shows the earthquake that shook southern Asia just before 8:00 am, local time. Most earthquakes, even major ones, last only a few seconds. These tremors went on for nearly ten minutes. When they subsided, no one realized that the earthquake had triggered something even more deadly—a tsunami.

Before a tsunami, the sea can recede by as much as 1.5 miles (2.5 km) on gently sloping shores

THE CALM BEFORE THE STRIKE
Up to half an hour before the tsunami struck, the ocean suddenly appeared to drain away from some beaches. When the trough—the low part of a wave—reaches the shore before the peak, it sucks the water offshore. This is called drawback and is an urgent warning to leave the beach. However, many people around the Indian Ocean went to investigate the exposed sand, with tragic results.

TIDE FLOODING SRI LANKA
This photograph, taken from a hotel room looking down on a beach resort in southwest Sri Lanka, shows the moment the massive wave struck, two hours after the earthquake. Waves up to 30 ft (10 m) high rushed in like a very strong, very fast tide, and kept coming, sweeping in between the buildings and trees.

TSUNAMI WAVE HIT PENANG

This still from an amateur video shows the moment the tsunami reached a tourist resort in Penang, Malaysia, 90 minutes after the earthquake. Fortunately, lifeguards at the tourist resorts had issued warnings to their guests to stay away from the beaches because of choppy waters. Malaysia was spared widespread disaster because the island of Sumatra shielded it from the tsunami's full force.

Oncoming water strikes wall and ricochets upward

Hour hand records the time when the tsunami struck

SWEPT OUT TO SEA

As the waves devastated the shores of Aceh province, many people were sucked out to sea and drowned. This young Indonesian man was swept away, but survived by clinging to a floating log. After nine days adrift, living on rainwater and coconuts, he was eventually picked up by a Malaysian container ship 100 miles (160 km) west of his home in Aceh.

TIME STOOD STILL

The first inhabited region to be struck was the city of Banda Aceh on the western tip of the island of Sumatra, Indonesia. This clock was found among the debris in Banda Aceh, stopped at 8:45 am, the time when the tsunami arrived. The waves were at their most destructive here, reaching a terrifying height of 80 ft (24 m).

RIVERS OF DEBRIS

At Patong Beach, on Phuket island, Thailand, a lone figure looks on as the water recedes, after waves traveled up to 1.2 miles (2 km) inland. There were thousands of casualties in Phuket, many receiving their injuries from the swirling debris unleashed by the onrush of the tsunami waves.

A drowned world

WHEN THE POUNDING WAVES STOPPED, as 2005 began, the survivors started to see the damage the Asian tsunami had wreaked. Exactly how many died in the disaster will never be known, since so many bodies were swept out to sea. The likely death toll is more than 200,000. Across the region, families separated by the tsunami searched anxiously for their loved ones. With roads and railroads washed away or covered in debris, many areas were completely cut off. People's lives were shattered as the tsunami demolished their homes, destroyed their fishing boats, flooded farmland with salt water, and left tourist resorts in ruins.

WRECKED BOATS, INDIA
Not only were lives lost in the tsunami, but livelihoods vanished, too. All around the Indian Ocean, fishing boats lay in heaps on the shore, many battered beyond repair, like these in the south Indian state of Tamil Nadu. The tsunami destroyed two-thirds of Tamil Nadu's fishing fleet.

Boats tossed around the buildings

WASHED AWAY
Worst hit on the east African coast was Somalia, 4,350 miles (7,000 km) from the epicenter. Three hundred Somalis died in towns hit by the waves, and 50,000 survivors needed food, shelter, and medical aid. In the district of Hafun, above, relief was held up because the tsunami had washed away the road into the town.

TWISTED TRACK
Near Sinigame, on the southwestern coast of Sri Lanka, 1,500 passengers perished when the full force of the tsunami hit the train they were traveling on. The waves not only swept the engine and cars from the track, but forced up the rails themselves, leaving a mass of twisted wood, metal, and tangled debris.

DESPERATE RESCUE
When the giant waves finally stopped coming, survivors waded into the sea, trying to rescue people who had been swept out by the force of the waves. All too often, the people they dragged from the water were already dead. Here, in the city of Madras on India's southern coast, 390 people lost their lives.

BANDA ACEH

The place most devastated by the tsunami's onslaught was the Indonesian city of Banda Aceh, on the island of Sumatra. The city was just 155 miles (250 km) from the earthquake's epicenter and, when the waves receded, it lay in ruins. Many eyewitnesses compared the ravaged city to Hiroshima in Japan, after the detonation of an atomic bomb in 1945. One hundred thousand people may have lost their lives in the Banda province in just 15 minutes.

Buildings utterly flattened

Fields contaminated with salty seawater. Crops may not be able to grow in them for years to come

MISSING PERSONS

For weeks after the disaster, notice boards in tourist resorts, such as the tropical island of Phuket, Thailand, were covered with photos of people who were still missing. With hospitals overflowing with the injured and dead, relatives and friends struggled to discover if their loved ones were dead or just lost in the confusion.

SALVAGING POSSESSIONS

Across the region, people picked through the remains of their shattered homes to salvage anything they could. Over a million people were left homeless by the tsunami. Here, in the remote Andaman and Nicobar Islands, clearing up was made more difficult by aftershocks from the earthquake, which continued for days after the tsunami.

Recovery begins

As the scale of the 2004 Asian disaster became apparent, aid began to arrive from around the globe. The first task was to provide shelter and medical assistance to survivors. Then local people and aid workers began to clear the debris left by the water. One of the most traumatic jobs was recovering the bodies of the victims before they started to rot and spread disease. Once the clearing operations were over, people could start getting back to their normal lives, going to school and to their jobs. The economy of much of this region relies heavily on tourism, so it was vital to attract visitors back to the area, by showing them that the tsunami had not destroyed a beautiful tropical paradise.

IN MEMORY OF THE DEAD
This Buddhist statue was left on the beach at Khao Lak, Thailand, in memory of those who had died in the disaster. Religious services for the victims were held on beaches all around the coast.

Refugee camp at Bang Muang, Phang Tha, in Thailand

AID RESCUE TEAM
Governments and aid agencies from around the world sent food, medicine, temporary shelters, and emergency supplies for those who had lost their homes and belongings. Among the rescue teams were hundreds of medical workers, such as this Chinese doctor. They cared for tens of thousands of shocked and injured patients.

TENT CITY
Vast camps were set up to house people made homeless by the disaster. There were fears that unsanitary conditions in such huge refugee camps might lead to outbreaks of diseases such as cholera and typhoid. This was prevented by the swift action of local and national health services. Their first priority was that survivors had safe drinking water and food, the means to cook, essentials such as soap, and adequate sanitation.

Elephant handler wears mask as protection against the smell of decaying bodies

ELEPHANTS AT WORK
After the disaster, it was essential that corpses were buried quickly, to prevent outbreaks of disease. Thailand's elephants, usually employed in the logging or tourist industries, proved invaluable now. Elephants could reach areas inaccessible to even four-wheel-drive trucks. First, dogs were used to sniff out bodies, then the elephants could effortlessly nudge aside lumber, masonry, or fallen trees to reveal the corpses hidden beneath. They also carried out the grim task of transporting the bodies to burial sites.

CLEARING THE DAMAGE
Tourism is one of the most important industries in Southeast Asia. Beach resorts such as Phi Phi island in Thailand lay ruined and covered in debris. Bulldozers were sent in to clear the area and demolish unsafe buildings, so that the task of rebuilding could begin.

Temporary shelter for aid workers and their equipment

BOAT BUILDING
All around the coast, local people set to work to rebuild boats shattered by the waves, or to start again if the boats were beyond repair. Boats are vital to the region's fishing fleet, but many tourist resorts also use them to show visitors the region's coral reefs and rich marine life.

Boat-building on the beach at Phuket, Thailand

BACK TO SCHOOL
The tsunami badly damaged this primary school in Hikkaduwa, Sri Lanka. However, just two weeks after the disaster, children who survived returned to classes in the repaired building. One-third of those who died in the tsunami were children, who were much less able to resist the force of the waves than adults.

Tsunami warnings

Tsunami evacuation sign

T$_{HE}$ 2004 TSUNAMI struck the Indian Ocean without warning, taking almost all of its victims by surprise. In the Pacific Ocean, where tsunamis are more common, oceanographers monitor the ocean for possible tsunamis. Sirens and broadcasts warn people when a tsunami is approaching, and signs indicate safe evacuation sites, such as higher ground or the upper floors of a reinforced concrete building. Earthquake-monitoring equipment at the Pacific Tsunami Warning Center did register the Sumatran earthquake, which caused the tsunami, but there was no system for informing people on the Indian Ocean coasts. If a warning system had been in place, thousands of lives might have been saved.

Antenna for sending signals to satellite

TSUNAMI OBSERVATION
A sensor fixed to the ocean floor below this Japanese buoy measures the pressure of water above it. If a tsunami as small as 0.4 in (1 cm) passes over it, the water pressure changes and the sensor sends a signal to the buoy on the sea surface. The buoy then signals a satellite, which alerts Japan's Tsunami Early Warning Center.

Solar panels power the buoy

Gate raised to allow tall ships into the harbor

Massive gate weighs 925 tons

HOLDING BACK THE WAVES
This enormous floodgate in Nomazu Port, Japan, has a door 30 ft (9.3 m) high, which automatically shuts against tsunamis. It is triggered by a seismograph— an earthquake-measuring device—which senses the ground movements that could lead to a tsunami. Most of Japan's population live along the coast, so measures like this are vital to protect the crowded cities of this earthquake-prone region.

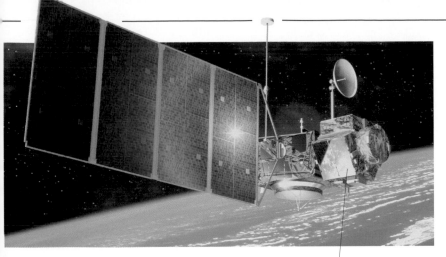

THE SEA FROM SPACE
Launched in 1992, the Poseidon satellite records the ocean currents and sea surface height from its orbit above Earth. Tiny fluctuations in sea level immediately after an undersea earthquake can give advance warning of a tsunami.

Two radar altimeters measure sea surface height

TSUNAMI WARNING TOWER
When the Warning Center spots an impending tsunami, the race is on to spread the news around coasts that may be affected. New warning towers, like this one in Thailand, are being built all around the Indian Ocean. The tower has a siren, and its antennae can interrupt TV and radio broadcasts to send text messages to warn the public that they should move to higher ground, away from the coast.

TSUNAMI WARNING CENTER
Oceanographers at the Pacific Tsunami Warning Center in Hawaii gather information about undersea earthquakes and sea level fluctuations to determine whether a tsunami is likely. Within half an hour of an earthquake, they can send out warnings, predicting where and when the tsunami will arrive. A similar warning system is being put in place around the Indian Ocean.

SONAR DEVICE
The first step in establishing an Indian Ocean tsunami warning system is to begin monitoring earthquake activity on the seabed in the region. This sonar device is being launched to map the seabed near Banda Aceh, where the 2004 tsunami originated. It will reflect sound off the seabed and build up a 3-D image.

Tourists relax in front of the Tsunami Warning Tower at Phuket, Thailand

Land areas above sea level

Steep slope leading to ocean depths

Areas below sea level are blue/green

THE OCEAN FLOOR IN 3-D
This false-color 3-D image of the ocean floor around California was made using sonar. Sonar maps like this enable oceanographers to study the contours of the seabed. Regular scanning reveals seabed movement, which could signal tsunami-triggering events. Such movement includes shifts along a fault line, or the collapse of unstable undersea slopes at the edges of continents.

Earth shakes

THE SURFACE OF OUR PLANET seems solid and unmoving——but Earth's plates are moving all the time, sometimes gently and gradually, and sometimes with a sudden jolt that makes the ground shake. Earthquakes are usually measured using a scale devised in 1935 by Charles Richter. The smallest recorded quakes measure up to 3.5 on the Richter scale, a degree of ground movement that may be just enough to rattle a cup on a table. The most severe earthquakes measure over 8 and can destroy entire cities. Earthquakes cannot be prevented, but scientists can study the records of past quakes and measure the buildup of stresses within the rocks. Then they can forecast the probability that a substantial earthquake will happen within a certain time.

POSEIDON THE EARTH-SHAKER
In ancient Greece, people believed that earthquakes were caused by the god of the sea, Poseidon. When he was angry, Poseidon stamped on the ground or stuck Earth with his three-pronged trident, and set off an earthquake. His unpredictable, violent behavior earned Poseidon the name "Earth-Shaker."

SAN ANDREAS FAULT
Like many fault lines, the San Andreas fault line generates many earthquakes. Extending 750 miles (1,200 km) through central California, it divides the Pacific and North American tectonic plates, and causes frequent earth tremors in the cities of San Francisco and Los Angeles. Some parts of the fault slip in regular jerks that produce slight tremors, while others get jammed and then shift as pressure is released, causing a major earthquake.

Fault line, where two of Earth's plates meet

Two plates moving in opposite directions

Epicenter, directly above focus

Seismic waves rippling from focus

Focus, where an earthquake begins

SEISMIC WAVES
When a fault sticks instead of sliding smoothly, massive forces build up underground until suddenly the rocks fracture at a point called the focus. Vibrations called seismic waves ripple outward from here. The force of the earthquake is greatest at the epicenter, directly above the focus on Earth's surface. The most damaging earthquakes have a focus less than 40 miles (65 km) beneath Earth's surface.

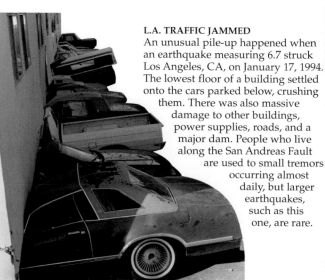

L.A. TRAFFIC JAMMED
An unusual pile-up happened when an earthquake measuring 6.7 struck Los Angeles, CA, on January 17, 1994. The lowest floor of a building settled onto the cars parked below, crushing them. There was also massive damage to other buildings, power supplies, roads, and a major dam. People who live along the San Andreas Fault are used to small tremors occurring almost daily, but larger earthquakes, such as this one, are rare.

MEXICO CITY QUAKE
When an earthquake measuring 8.1 hit Mexico City on September 19, 1985, buildings up to 15 stories high began to swing like pendulums. Nearly 9,000 people died, most of them crushed inside collapsing buildings. Rescue workers were hampered in their efforts to free people by smaller aftershocks. These shocks follow a big earthquake as rocks settle into new positions, and can bring down buildings already damaged in the main quake.

EARTHQUAKE DETECTOR
In AD 132, Chinese astronomer Zhang Heng invented the first seismoscope, a device for detecting ground movement. This bronze device shows the direction a tremor comes from, and works within a range of about 400 miles (600 km).

Earth tremors cause one of the dragons to release a ball

Colored bands are narrow around the epicenter, showing greater land displacement

Epicenter of earthquake

Ball falls into open mouth of toad below

Toad farthest from epicenter catches the ball. The quake lies in the opposite direction of that of the toad

Fault line

Fine needle moves with the tremors, recording the vibrations with ink

The greater the shock wave, the wider the zigzag on the display

REVEALING QUAKES
Earth tremors can be detected, recorded, and measured using a seismograph, such as this portable device. Seismographs can detect vibrations called foreshocks that are produced by deep rocks fracturing before an earthquake. Monitoring foreshocks helps scientists to predict earthquakes.

GROUND MOVEMENTS
This satellite radar image shows movements of land following an earthquake measuring 7.1 in California in 1999. The colored bands represent contours. The distance between adjacent contours of the same color indicate 4 in (10 cm) of ground displacement.

Surviving a quake

ENGINEERS SAY that it is not earthquakes that kill, but buildings. Earthquakes usually have a minor impact in the wilderness, but when they affect built-up areas, the results can be devastating. In some earthquake zones, buildings are specially constructed to absorb vibrations without collapsing. But even supposedly earthquake-proof cities may come crashing down in a major quake. When an earthquake does strike, emergency plans are put into action. Trained teams are despatched to rescue the injured from the rubble, evacuate victims from danger zones, fight fires, make ruined buildings safe, and, eventually, restore essential services.

FIGHTING FIRE
After the ground has stopped shaking, damage to electrical equipment and gas pipes can lead to an outbreak of fires. Firefighters have to struggle through the ruined buildings and broken roads to reach the blaze. In Kobe, Japan, many of the city's ancient wooden buildings burned down when firefighters ran out of water.

CITY IN RUINS
The ancient fortress, or citadel, of Arg-e Bam stood on a hill overlooking the city of Bam in Iran for 11 centuries, until December 27, 2003. The violent earthquake that hit Bam that day flattened the modern city, as well as the mud brick fortress and other historic buildings dating back to the 16th and 17th centuries. More than 26,000 people died and 70,000 were left homeless.

THE CITADEL OF ARG-E BAM IN 2003

THE CITADEL OF ARG-E BAM IN 2004

Shaking caused the loose ground to move like a liquid, and it could no longer support the freeway

SHOCK IN JAPAN
During the earthquake that struck the city of Kobe, Japan, on January 17, 1995, bolts holding together elevated (built above ground) roads snapped, sending sections of road crashing to the ground. Much of Kobe is built on ground that becomes unstable during an earthquake. Also, the epicenter of the 6.9- magnitude earthquake was only 12 miles (20 km) from the city. Its shock waves damaged or destroyed some 140,000 buildings and claimed the lives of 5,500 people.

EMERGENCY SHELTER
An earthquake victim is given a medical checkup in an evacuation center. One month after Kobe's earthquake, 226,000 people were living in centers like this one. Some 300,000 people lost their homes and the authorities were unable to accommodate all of them. Some had to sleep in tents or in their cars in freezing winter weather.

Earphones, for listening for signs of life

SEARCHING FOR LIFE
When an earthquake hits a city, people can be buried alive inside collapsed buildings. It is vital that rescuers find them quickly before they suffocate or die of their injuries, or perish from lack of water and food. Rescuers may use a trapped person detector, like this one. The device can detect vibrations as faint as those from a heartbeat, letting rescuers know if anyone is alive in the rubble.

Microphone, for amplifying sounds from vibrations

Sensor, for picking up vibrations

Subsensors, can be placed in different parts of a building

Cable coil, to enable sensors to be moved around so that every part of a building can be investigated

COMBING THE RUBBLE
Trained dogs can help rescue workers by sniffing out survivors in the rubble of a collapsed building. Dogs have the added advantage that they can move lightly over loose material, while a person's weight could disturb the rubble and cause more debris to fall on anyone trapped below.

Mighty volcanoes

GODDESS PELE
According to legend, the Hawaiian goddess of volcanoes, Pele, has all the powers of a volcano. She is said to make mountains, melt rocks, destroy forests, and build new islands.

Underneath Earth's solid crust lie pockets of burning hot molten rock called magma. Less dense than the rock above it, magma rises to the surface through weak spots in the crust. Most of these weaknesses lie along the margins of Earth's tectonic plates, but a few are found at hot spots (areas of deep heat within Earth) far from the plate edges, such as the Hawaiian islands and Yellowstone. As the magma pushes upward, pressure builds until the magma breaks through Earth's crust, sending rock, ash, and lava cascading or oozing onto the surface as a volcano.

SLEEPING VOLCANO
Japan's beautiful Mount Fuji last erupted in 1707 and is now classed as dormant. Dormant volcanoes show no signs of activity, but they may erupt in the future. Active volcanoes erupt constantly, or with gaps of a few years. Volcanoes that have been dormant for thousands of years are called extinct—although scientists cannot be certain that they will never erupt again.

Ashy steam blasting from the volcano's vent

BIRTH OF AN ISLAND
The majority of volcanic eruptions take place under the oceans. In 1963, an undersea eruption occurred off the coast of Iceland, with unusual results. The sea began to steam as seawater poured into the volcano's vent and was boiled by its heat. Over the next three and a half years, lava and ash from the volcano piled up, eventually forming an entirely new island, Surtsey, measuring 1 sq mile (2.5 sq km) in area.

FIERY RIVER
When the magma inside a volcano is runny and does not contain much gas, it oozes or gushes from the volcano in a hot stream of lava, like this pahoehoe (pah-hoy-hoy) lava in Hawaii. When the magma is thick and sticky, it traps gases such as steam and carbon dioxide inside it. Sticky, viscous magma erupts from the volcano in a violent explosion of lava globules and burning ash.

Molten lava sets fire to trees

Cracks and ridges form as the top of the lava sheet hardens

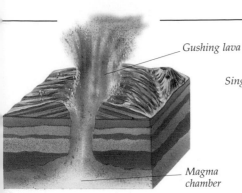

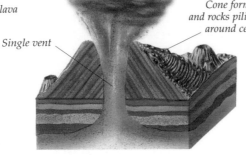

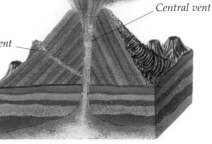

SHIELD CONE VOLCANO
Runny lava escapes from the volcano's vent (opening) in a fountain or a gushing river. This type of lava runs easily along the ground, spreading over a wide area. Successive eruptions form a massive mountain with gently sloping sides. A typical shield cone volcano is Mauna Kea, Hawaii.

Gushing lava

Magma chamber

CINDER CONE VOLCANO
This erupts ash and rocky material, which falls in a ring. These volcanoes usually have only one vent. The straight-sided, cone-shaped crater is created by the rocks and rock fragments from many eruptions. Cinder cones, such as Paricutin, Mexico, rarely rise more than 1,000 ft (300 m) above land.

Single vent

Cone formed by ash and rocks piling steeply around central vent

STRATOVOLCANO
The lava is thick and sticky, so it cools and hardens quickly, producing a steep, symmetrical mountain. Eruptions of lava alternate with rocky and ashy material, producing distinct layers in the mountain. Stratovolcanoes may grow as high as 8,000 ft (2,500 m), and can be cone- or dome-shaped.

Side vent

Central vent

TAKING THE TEMPERATURE
Volcanologists (scientists who study volcanoes) can find out what is going on beneath Earth's surface by measuring the ground temperature around volcanic vents. Active volcanoes have to be monitored frequently, so that people can be warned when an eruption is likely. If the ground temperature rises, it may be a warning of an impending eruption.

TAKING SAMPLES
After eruptions, volcanologists dressed in heat-protective suits collect fresh lava samples for analysis. They have to work fast, since further eruptions are always possible. Lava samples can provide information about changes in a volcano's behavior. For example, scientists may analyze the mixture of gases in the lava to see if they have become more explosive.

Rivers of fire

THE DEVASTATING POWER of an exploding volcano is a magnificent and terrifying sight. As the volcanic cone comes unplugged, enormous pressures are released, forcing lava, ash, rocks, and superheated gases out. After an eruption, people may return to farm the soil nearby, particularly if it is now nourished with mineral-rich volcanic ash. Fortunately, today most eruptions can be predicted and people can be evacuated from the danger zone. However, the effects of a volcanic eruption can reach far wider than the foot of the mountain. A major eruption can affect the weather over the whole world.

Plume of volcanic ash

MOUNT ST. HELENS
When Mount St. Helens, Washington, erupted on May 18, 1980, a column of gas, ash, and pumice was sent hurtling 15 miles (24 km) into the atmosphere. So much rock was blown off the top of the mountain that it lost 1,350 ft (400 m) in height. A cloud of ash spread over an area of 20,000 sq miles (50,000 sq km), causing a major hazard for aircraft.

Uprooted and burned fir trees

AFTER THE ERUPTION
The Mount St. Helens eruption flattened around 230 sq miles (600 sq km) of forest, and wiped out virtually all the local wildlife. Scientists estimate that it will take 200 years for the forest to return to its pre-eruption condition.

JETS OF FIRE
In 2001, Italy's Mount Etna exploded with a bang. Rising 11,120 ft (3,390 m) above the island of Sicily, Etna is one of Europe's highest mountains, and its most active volcano. Usually it erupts in small, continuous bursts like a firework display. Local people fight a constant battle with lava flows that damage roads, buildings, farmland, and threaten towns. Concrete barriers, trenches, even explosives have been used in attempts to redirect the lava, but with limited success.

Fern

Lichen

Moss

NEW LIFE
After a volcanic eruption, the first plants to appear in solidified lava are mosses, lichens, and small weeds. It may take decades for the volcanic rock to break down into fertile soil. Once this happens, larger plants begin to take root.

PYROCLASTIC FLOW

After 600 years lying dormant, on June 15, 1991, Mount Pinatubo in the Philippines began erupting. A gigantic column of rock particles and ash was ejected 25 miles (40 km) into the atmosphere. As the column collapsed, this deadly cloud of hot gas and debris, called a pyroclastic flow, hurtled at speeds of 100 mph (160 km/h) across the surrounding area. Haze spread around the globe, blocking out some sunlight

DEADLY DUST

As ash from Mount Pinatubo filled the air with a choking cloud and covered the fields, farmers took their buffalo to look for unaffected areas. Many survivors developed pneumonia from inhaling the gritty ash, and entire harvests were lost.

PANIC IN POMPEII

The prosperous Roman town of Pompeii lay in the shadow of Italy's Mount Vesuvius. The volcano had been dormant for centuries, so the townspeople were taken by surprise when they felt the first rumbles of an eruption on August 24, a d 79. This artist's impression shows the pyroclastic flow about to engulf the town.

Ash around the bodies hardened, preserving the shapes of the dead

DEADLY DUST

Many people managed to escape from Pompeii, but some 2,000 were trapped in the town. They died of suffocation as a choking pyroclastic flow swept through the streets. Pompeii and its dead were buried under 100 ft (30 m) of ash, and not discovered until excavations began in 1860.

Fluid lava pours down the slopes

Landslides and avalanches

** O**NE TYPE OF NATURAL DISASTER can happen in any part of the world. Wherever a steep hillside is found, when the pull of gravity is greater than the forces that hold together the particles on the slope, a mass of loose material may come crashing down the slope. On a rocky or muddy hillside, unstable rocks and soil can cause a landslide. On a snowy mountainside, snow can hurtle as an avalanche, burying people and buildings in its path. Speedy rescue is essential to save any survivors buried under the dense snow or masses of rocks and mud. For hundreds of years, rescue teams have used dogs to find trapped people.

Saint Bernard rescue dog

AVALANCHE WARNING SIGN
In mountain ski resorts, such as the Swiss Alps and the Rockies in the US and Canada, warning signs indicate the risk of avalanches. Although it is difficult to predict exactly when and where an avalanche will take place, experts can tell when the snow layers begin to become unstable enough to trigger an avalanche.

TO THE RESCUE
High in the mountains, rescue teams use helicopters to reach injured people quickly. A winch is used to lower rescuers and haul up the injured on stretchers. The pilot must be very careful, since even the noise and rotor wash of a helicopter can trigger a further avalanche.

TORRENT OF SNOW
An avalanche starts when mountain snow builds into an unstable overhang or becomes loose because of a thaw. Triggered by an earth tremor or by a loud noise, the avalanche grows as it rolls down the slope, loosening more snow and picking up rocks and soil. The path of an avalanche can be half a mile (800 m) wide. Anyone caught up in it has just a 5 percent chance of survival.

AVALANCHE PREVENTION
Fences built across the slopes can bring tumbling snow to a halt before it has a chance to grow into a huge avalanche. Sometimes explosives are used to trigger small, controlled avalanches. This prevents the buildup of large snow masses that could cause a major avalanche.

TYPES OF LANDSLIDES

There are four types of landslides. Soil creep is a slow movement—as its name suggests—due to tiny shifts in the soil particles. Slumping is a faster slide, occurring when slabs of land slip down a slope. Debris flow happens when a slope becomes saturated with water and triggers a landslide of a water-soaked mass of soil and rocks. Rockfalls are sudden slides caused by heavy rain or frost dislodging larger rock pieces.

Steep, water-saturated slope

Loose pieces of rock

Rockfall

Debris flow

Slumping

Soil creep

ROCKY ROAD

In August 1983, an 18-ft (6-m) slab of granite crashed down from the hillside onto the highway in Yosemite National Park, California. Rockfalls along roads are often the result of poor construction methods. Road builders may cut into hillsides without supporting them properly, or build on slopes that are too steep.

SLIPPING INTO THE SEA

The coast can be a dangerous place to build. In 1993, the clay slope beneath this hotel in Scarborough, UK, became saturated with water and slumped into the sea, taking part of the building with it. Even solid stone cliffs can be eroded by wind-driven rain and waves until the clifftop is left overhanging precariously.

Part of hotel reduced to landslide rubble

Rescue workers carry the body of a landslide victim

DEADLY DEBRIS

An earthquake measuring 7.6 on the Richter scale hit San Salvador, El Salvador, on January 13, 2001. It triggered a massive debris flow in the Santa Tecla neighborhood. Soil and rocks swept down the hillside, cutting straight through the streets and homes below. Buildings directly in the path of the debris flow were flattened, killing 63 people.

Earth's atmosphere

LAYERS OF THE ATMOSPHERE
The atmosphere is divided into four distinct layers based on temperature and humidity. The outermost layer, the thermosphere, is the thickest, extending into space. Gravity keeps most of the atmosphere's water and air in the lowest layer, the troposphere. The Sun's rays pass through the outer atmosphere to warm the air and water, causing them to move. These movements make the planet's weather.

Some satellites orbit at the top of the thermosphere

THE ATMOSPHERE IS A BAND OF GASES—mostly nitrogen, oxygen, and argon—held around Earth by gravity. Air masses, each defined by fairly uniform temperature and humidity, move around the atmosphere. The interaction of air masses creates all the conditions that make up the weather—from clear, sunny skies to hurricanes and torrential rain. The pattern of weather over time in a particular region is called the climate. In some parts of the world, extreme weather conditions are part of the climate. In other places, the climate is less extreme, so people are totally unprepared when a weather disaster strikes.

Aurora, the Northern and Southern Lights, occur in the lower thermosphere

4. Thermosphere begins here. It thins out into space at about 400 miles (650 km) above Earth's surface

Most meteors burn up by the time they reach the mesosphere

3. Mesosphere extends up to about 50 miles (80 km) above Earth's surface

2. Stratosphere, reaching up to about 28 miles (48 km) above Earth's surface. Contains ozone, which absorbs some of the Sun's ultraviolet radiation before it reaches Earth's surface

1. Troposphere, up to 12 miles (19 km) above Earth's surface. The planet's weather happens within this level

THUNDERCLOUDS IN THE ATMOSPHERE
Viewed from space, the atmosphere looks like a light haze around the planet. Just above Earth's surface, in the troposphere, vast thunderclouds are silhouetted against the orange setting sun. The blue color of the sky is caused by sunlight scattered by molecules of nitrogen, oxygen, and water in the air. The layers in the blue sky in this picture were created by volcanic ash from eruptions at Mount Pinatubo, in the Philippines, and Mount Spurr, Alaska.

SOARING CLOUDS
Clouds form in the lowest layer of the atmosphere, the troposphere. Towering cumulonimbus storm clouds like this one can reach 15 miles (24 km) high, and punch through the top of the troposphere. The largest storm clouds can contain 275,000 tons of water. These clouds produce thunderstorms, hailstorms, tornadoes, torrential rain, and snow.

Wind moves in three circuits, or cells, on each side of the equator

The equator

High-level winds

Surface winds

Polar easterlies, which blow from the east in the polar region

In the middle circuits, surface winds move toward the poles

Direction of Earth's rotation

Westerly winds, which blow from the west

Northeast trades—in the days of sailing ships, trading ships relied on these winds

Near the equator, prevailing surface winds generally move toward the equator

WHAT IS WIND?

The Sun warms the land and sea, which warms the air above. Warm air has low density, so it rises and cold, high-density air moves in to take its place. This movement of air is what we know as wind. Prevailing winds (winds that blow fairly steadily from one direction) are arranged in a series of bands, or circuits, around the globe.

MAPPING THE WEATHER

On this weather map, lines called isobars link areas with equal air pressure. Air pressure is the weight of air pressing down on a given area. High pressure brings cloudless blue skies, while low pressure brings wet, stormy weather. Spiked and bumped lines on the map show the fronts (boundaries) of air masses. When air masses collide, they bring a change of weather along the front.

High-pressure area

Closely spaced isobars indicate a strong wind

Spiked line indicates a cold front

Bumped lines indicate a warm front

Low-pressure area

1028

1024

1036

1044

996

1006

980

Spiked and bumped lines show cold and warm fronts meeting

Isobar joins points of equal air pressure

ICE STORM

In parts of North America, ice storms can cover the landscape with a coating of clear ice. Ice storms happen when snow melts as it falls through a layer of warm air, then supercools as it hits cold air nearer the ground. In 1998, an ice storm covered much of Quebec, Canada, including the city of Montreal. The ice storm became the most expensive natural disaster in Canada's history, as the weight of clinging ice brought down so many power lines that four million people were left without electricity.

DESERT DUST STORM

In dry desert landscapes, hot, high-pressure air sits steadily over the land, bringing clear skies with temperatures as high as 140°F (60°C) in the daytime and below freezing at night. Occasionally, moist winds sweep across the desert, mix with the hot air, and rise high into the atmosphere. There, they cool to form huge thunderclouds that bring short, violent thunderstorms. The now cool, dry air falls to the ground and spreads out, creating a wind up to 60 mph (100 km/h), which whips up dusty soil to form a swirling dust storm, like this one in Iraq.

Wild weather

At any time, across the world, about 2,000 thunderstorms are lighting up the sky with giant electrical sparks. A bolt of lightning can reach 54,000°F (30,000°C), five times hotter than the surface of the Sun. The massive electrical charge a lightning bolt carries can kill in an instant. Most thunderstorms happen in summer, when warm air rises to form thunderclouds. These storms can bring torrential rain or stinging hail. Meteorologists track the path of thunderstorms using information from satellites, weather stations on the ground, and specially adapted weather planes that can fly into storms.

EIFFEL TOWER STRUCK
This dramatic photograph shows lightning striking the Eiffel Tower in Paris, France. Like other tall buildings, the Eiffel Tower is protected from damage from lightning strikes by a lightning conductor—a metal cable or strap that leads the electrical charge down to the ground where it discharges harmlessly.

THUNDER AND LIGHTNING
Inside a storm cloud, water droplets and ice crystals rise and fall violently, building up a massive static electrical charge. The charge sends a spark of lightning to the ground, creating fork lightning, or among the clouds, making sheet lightning. The air around the lightning heats up and expand, creating a shock wave that is heard as a clap of thunder.

2. Warm, moist air rises over cool air and forms clouds

3. Persistent rain or drizzle falls

1. Warm air rises and meets cool air

Frontal cloud

2. Warm, moist air rises, mixes, or converges, and cools to form clouds

3. Clouds release their moisture as rain showers or brief storms

1. Warm ground heats the air

4. Cool air sinks

Convergence cloud

HOW RAINCLOUDS FORM
The Sun's heat makes water from the oceans and on land evaporate into the air. The moist, warm air rises and becomes cooler. As it cools, the water vapor in it condenses to form clouds. The water droplets in the cloud link together and grow heavier. When the cloud is thick enough, the water falls back to Earth as rain, hail, or snow. Factors that make warm, moist air rise rapidly, creating storm clouds, occur where one air mass overrides another (frontal wedging), where air converges, and where mountains uplift moving air.

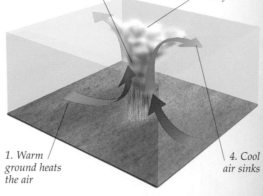

3. Far slopes are left dry

2. Clouds form and fall as rain

1. Warm air rises and cools as it meets the mountain

Mountain lifting

FLYING INTO THE STORM

Airplanes such as this WC-130 Hercules are used to monitor weather in the US. Similar planes are used around the world. When severe weather is expected, such planes can fly into the storm to analyze the speed, strength, and direction of the wind. Meteorologists use this information to predict which areas will be struck by the storm and how badly.

Radar equipment in nose of plane

Tubes show the branching path of the lightning

LIGHTNING SCULPTURE

This weird sculpture of solidified sand was created by lightning. As lightning passes through sand, it heats up the sand grains to melting point and then fuses them together to form a structure of hollow tubes, called a fulgurite. Lightning's intense heat can ignite trees and wooden buildings, causing natural fires.

Thunderclouds over Gillette, Wyoming

BLACK CLOUDS AND HAIL

Hailstones form when raindrops, moving up and down in the freezing air inside black thunderclouds, become coated with layers of ice. Large hailstones can be bigger than a baseball, but most are the size of a pea. Even when they are tiny, these balls of ice can cause havoc, battering fields of crops, damaging property, and turning roads into hazardous, slippery ice-skating rinks.

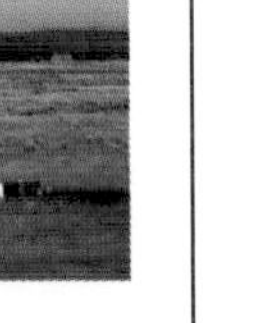

Baseball

Giant hailstone

Hurricane force

Storm at sea

IN LATE SUMMER, above the warm, tropical seas that lie on either side of the equator, enormous rotating storm systems can develop with wind speeds of 75 mph (120 km/h) and above. These storms are called hurricanes when they originate over the Atlantic Ocean, cyclones in the Indian Ocean, and typhoons in the Pacific. The biggest measure 300–500 miles (500–800 km) across. These storms can travel thousands of miles, sweeping inland from the ocean, and leaving a trail of destruction. High winds toss boats around, uproot trees, and topple buildings, while torrential rain and surges of seawater bring devastating floods.

BLOWN OVER
This tree's strange shape was caused by the fierce wind off the sea constantly pushing it in one direction as it grew. Winds are stronger over the oceans than on land because there are no obstacles to slow them down. Strong ocean breezes batter coastlines, then gradually run out of energy as they move inland.

HURRICANE FORMING
This satellite image shows spiral bands of cloud forming Hurricane Ivan, as it passes over the Cayman Islands in the Atlantic Ocean in September 2004. For a hurricane to form, the temperature of the sea must be above 80°F (27°C), fueling wind speeds greater than 74 mph (118 km/h). A hurricane can pick up two billion tons of water vapor from the sea each day, to be dumped on land as torrential rain.

Blue arrows show cool air spiraling outward at top of hurricane

Dry air sinks into the eye of the storm

Eye area

Air spirals inward at bottom of hurricane

The fastest winds and heaviest rain spiral around the low-pressure eye wall

Sea surface bulges in the low-pressure eye area

Red arrows show spiraling bands of wind and rain

INSIDE A HURRICANE
A hurricane is created by an area of warm air rising above the ocean, and sucking in surrounding air. Earth's rotation makes the air spin. As the spinning air rises, it cools, creating a spiral of towering storm clouds. At the center of the hurricane is an area of calm air known as the eye.

The calm eye of the storm

Thick clouds spiral around the eye

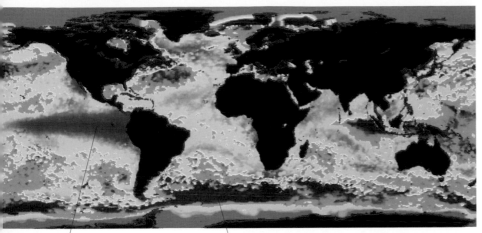

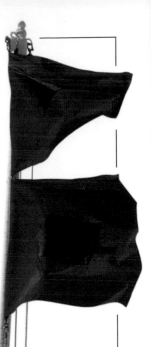

EL NIÑO
Every three to seven years, a weather pattern called El Niño causes winds over the Pacific to temporarily change direction. This colored satellite image shows the difference between the normal sea temperatures worldwide and those that occurred during the 1997 El Niño event. The winds push warm water toward South America, bringing hurricanes and other tropical storms, while countries to the west of the ocean may experience drought.

Red shows sea temperatures farthest above normal

Purple shows sea temperatures farthest below normal

EYE OF THE STORM
Hurricane Fran's fiercest wind and most torrential rain batter a gas station in North Carolina in 1996. The most violent part of the hurricane often follows a calm period, when it might seem that the storm has passed. In the midst of the whirling wind and rain, the sky may suddenly clear and the air grow still, as the eye of the storm passes. A few moments later, the storm returns with renewed vigor.

HURRICANE WARNINGS
Flags like these alert residents and ships when a hurricane is approaching the coast. Weather forecasters also broadcast an advance warning called a weather watch on television, radio, and the Internet, telling people to look and listen for updates. Once the storm is certain to strike, a severe weather warning is broadcast. The best place to shelter is inside a brick or concrete building, far away from the windows.

WIND AND WAVES
In 1998, Hurricane Georges sent huge waves crashing onto the coast of Florida. When the eye passes over the coast, it brings with it a towering wall of water called a storm surge, which can reach 12 ft (3 m) high. This terrifying surge in sea level is caused by low air pressure at the storm's center, and it is responsible for many of the deaths that occur during hurricanes.

Palm trees bend but rarely break in hurricane winds

3. *Andrew over the
Gulf of Mexico, August 25*

2. *Andrew passing over
Florida, August 24*

1. *Hurricane Andrew
at sea, August 23, 1992*

Battling the wind

To **PREDICT** how a hurricane is going
to develop, meteorologists need to
measure its air pressure and wind
speed. Satellites can spot hurricanes
as they form, but the best way to
collect detailed, accurate pressure and
wind speed data is to send planes
known as Hurricane Hunters right
inside the hurricane. Even with all
this information, hurricane forecasting
can be tricky. When a hurricane
moves over land, it gradually runs
out of energy, but if it sweeps on out
to sea, warmth from the water can
speed up the wind once more. Every
year, around 90 hurricanes batter the
world's vulnerable coasts.

HURRICANE HUNTERS
During a 12-hour flight through
Hurricane Floyd in 1999, hurricane
hunters recorded wind speed,
humidity, and pressure in the
heart of the storm. The data was
sent to a weather station, where
a computer analyzed it to predict
the path of Floyd. Predictions give
a general guide, but hurricanes
can change direction unexpectedly.

*This infrared satellite image of
Hurricane Floyd helped the hurricane
hunters plan their flight path*

CAPSIZED YACHTS
One of the fiercest storms in
US history, Hurricane Andrew tore
through Florida in August 1992. A storm
surge 17 ft (5 m) high left yachts in Key
Biscayne's marina in a jumbled heap. The
storm weakened as it crossed Florida, but
then regained strength over the warm
waters of the Gulf of Mexico.

HURRICANE ANDREW
This sequence of satellite images shows the path of Hurricane Andrew as it traveled from east to west over three days in August 1992. Continuous wind speeds of 142 mph (228 km/h) with gusts up to 200 mph (321 km/h) were measured across Florida, before the force of the hurricane destroyed weather measuring devices. Andrew killed 26 people, although it narrowly missed the city of Miami, where many more lives could have been lost.

Wooden building, easily destroyed by a hurricane

THE GREAT STORM OF '87
In the middle of an October night in 1987, an unexpectedly severe storm hit southern Britain. As the storm brewed out in the Atlantic, it mixed with warm winds from the tail end of a hurricane. As a result, some of the wind gusts reached hurricane speeds of 122 mph (196 km/h). The storm toppled 15 million trees and caused severe damage to buildings.

CYCLONE TRACY
In the early hours of Christmas Day 1974, Cyclone Tracy struck the city of Darwin in northern Australia. Winds up to 135 mph (217 km/h) killed 65 people, and a further 16 were never found from the 22 vessels struck out at sea. After the storm, so many buildings lay in ruins that the city had to be almost entirely rebuilt.

Houseboat tipped over by massive waves

Trees uprooted by the force of the wind

PATH OF GEORGES, 1998
Holding on to each other to avoid being swept away by the 89-mph (144-km/h) wind, these men struggled to reach the shelter of a solid building as Hurricane Georges tore across Florida. By the time the storm reached the US, it had already ravaged the Caribbean, taking more than 600 lives and ruining much of the region's crops.

Hurricane Katrina

WHEN HURRICANE KATRINA hit the southern US in August 2005, more than 1,000 people died in the most destructive and costly natural disaster in US history. In the aftermath of the storm, over a million people were left homeless and five million without power. The streets of the historic city of New Orleans lay under yards of water. Evacuees from the region were taken to makeshift emergency shelters in neighboring states, or moved in with relatives and friends across the United States. Many said they were unlikely ever to return to the region where this catastrophic disaster had struck.

COURSE OF KATRINA
Hurricane Katrina passed over the Bahamas, south Florida, Louisiana, Mississippi, and Alabama between August 23 and 31, 2005. The wind reached a steady speed of 175 mph (280 km/h) with even stronger gusts. Katrina produced a storm surge that crashed onto a stretch of coastline over 200 miles (300 km) long. The wind finally began to lose strength and dropped below hurricane speed 150 miles (240 km) inland, near Jackson, Mississippi.

STORM SURGE
As the eye of the hurricane moved across the coast of Mississippi, it created a storm surge nearly 30 ft (10 m) high. In the town of Long Beach, cars and rubble were swept along by the surge, and dumped in a towering heap against the side of a building.

Tuba is too valuable to leave behind

LEAVING HOME
On August 28, with Hurricane Katrina heading for New Orleans, the city's mayor ordered everybody to evacuate. Five days after the storm, New Orleans was almost completely deserted. With electricity and water cut off and no food supplies, the last evacuees left their homes, clutching a few precious possessions.

UNDERWATER CITY
Rising floodwaters breached three of the levees—massive embankments—that were designed to protect New Orleans from flooding. By August 30, a day after Katrina hit the city, 80 percent of New Orleans was flooded. Some areas lay under 20 ft (6 m) of water. It took three weeks to repair the levees and pump the water out.

BROKEN WINDOWS

Curtains dangle outside hotel windows smashed by the force of Hurricane Katrina. Beds were seen flying out of the windows of one hotel. However, modern concrete and steel buildings like this one survived relatively unscathed. Many of New Orleans's famous wooden buildings, particularly those in the historic French Quarter, were completely destroyed. A commission was set up to advise the city government on how best to rebuild, taking into account the views and needs of all New Orleans's citizens.

Clear eye of the storm

Strong eye-wall winds

BOAT RESCUE

Hundreds of thousands of New Orleans residents were left behind when the hurricane struck. Many of them gathered in evacuation centers to await rescue. After the storm, rescuers arrived in boats to pick up the people who were stranded and searched from house to house to check for other survivors.

A solitary car travels toward the city as most residents rush to leave

FLEEING HURRICANE RITA

Three weeks after Katrina, warnings of the arrival of Hurricane Rita sent residents of cities such as Houston, Texas, rushing to evacuate, fearing for their lives. Mass evacuations like this bring hazards of their own, as panicking drivers may cause accidents on the jammed roads. Fortunately, Hurricane Rita turned out to be much less severe than Katrina.

Twisting tornadoes

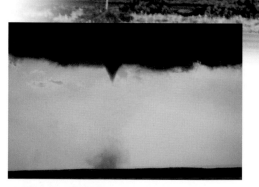

THE MOST VIOLENT WINDS on Earth, tornadoes (sometimes nicknamed twisters) can travel across the land at speeds up to 125 mph (200 km/h). They can lift objects as large as trains and hurl them to the ground, rip roofs off houses and whip out the furniture, suck up papers and photographs and drop them dozens of miles away, and even strip the clothes off a person's body. Tornadoes have hit every state in the US, but most of the world's tornadoes happen in the open prairies of the Midwest. There, the tornado season normally lasts from May to October.

FLYING FISH
Tornadoes passing over lakes and sea may suck up fish and frogs, then drop them on dry land.

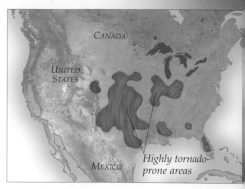

TORNADO ALLEY
In the center of the United States is an area known as Tornado Alley. It covers parts of Kansas, Oklahoma, and Missouri—the Plains. In the summer, cold air from Canada underrides warm, moist air from the Gulf of Mexico and hot, dry air from the Plains, causing great atmospheric instability. Eighty percent of the world's tornadoes occur here.

Tower of cloud called a thunderhead tops the supercell

STORM CLOUDS
When a huge, dark storm cloud known as a supercell fills the sky, a tornado may be on the way. Strong winds moving in different directions inside the cloud create a region of low pressure beneath the cloud. Warm, moist air rushes into the updraft and rises to meet cold air higher up. The two air masses turn around each other to form a wide column of air called a mesocyclone.

Revolving mesocyclone sucks up dust from the ground

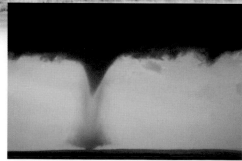

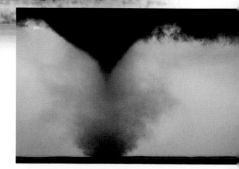

1 FUNNEL APPEARS
The first signs of a mesocyclone are swirling dust at ground level and a funnel of water vapor extending down from the cloud. As warm, moist air from the atmosphere is sucked into the base of the mesocyclone, it spins upward, carrying dust with it.

2 COLUMN FORMS
The warm air rises and cools, forming water vapor that joins the swirling funnel. When the funnel touches the ground, it becomes a tornado. As the tornado sucks up more dust, and more warm air cools to become water vapor, the tornado becomes clearly visible.

3 DYING DOWN
The tornado slows down as it runs out of moist, warm air at the bottom, or when cool, dry air sinks from the cloud. Tornadoes can last from a few seconds to an hour or more, but most last about three minutes.

TERRIFYING TWISTER

Inside the tornado's column, air whirls inward and upward, creating a flow called a vortex, at up to 300 mph (500 km/h)—double the speed of the most powerful hurricanes. Pressure inside the vortex is so low that the twister sucks up items beneath it, like a vacuum cleaner. Tornadoes rarely travel more than 6 miles (10 km) before they run out of energy, but one twister may trigger another, leading to a terrifying tornado outbreak.

DUST DEVIL

As air rises in the hot desert, it can create a draft that begins to swirl, just like a tornado. This tower of whirling dust and sand, known as a dust devil, can reach 1.2 miles (2 km) high. Dust devils are less fierce than tornadoes, with wind speeds reaching only about 60 mph (100 km/h).

Wind speed is faster in narrow parts of the column

TORNADO DAMAGE

When people emerge from their homes after a tornado has passed through, they may find everything flattened. Ruined vehicles lie around, crushed by falling debris, or smashed by the twister. Trees can be snapped in two, and power lines trail from broken poles. Flimsy mobile homes are particularly at risk from tornado damage.

STORM-CHASERS

When a severe storm develops, scientists known as storm-chasers follow the storm to monitor its progress. A Doppler radar mounted on a truck allows them to watch for a vortex developing inside the storm clouds. But even storm-chasers cannot predict a tornado more than 24 hours in advance.

WATERSPOUT

A tornado over the sea or a lake contains a column of condensed water, forming a pale waterspout. Although the wind speeds inside a waterspout are usually less than a tornado, the vortex is still powerful enough to lift a boat right out of the water.

Flood alert

WATER IS VITAL to survival—for drinking, washing, and growing crops. Rivers and seas provide food and transport links to other places. But when a river bursts its banks, or huge storm waves sweep in from the sea, water becomes a deadly enemy. The force of the flooding river or sea can sweep away people and animals, and flatten poorly constructed buildings. In a historic city, buildings that have stood for centuries can be damaged, and valuable artworks destroyed. In steep landscapes, torrential rain can lead to a flash flood—a deadly surge of water that rises so rapidly that it can catch people completely unprepared.

RAINY SEASON
In India, children often celebrate the first rains of the monsoon season. The monsoon usually starts with a dramatic thunderstorm and torrential rain lasting several days. In spite of the flooding it brings, the monsoon is eagerly awaited, as it signals the end of the hot, humid season, and provides water for thirsty crops.

Floodplain of lower Nile River

FERTILE FLOODPLAINS
The ancient Egyptians depended on the Nile's annual flood across its flood plain—the flat land on either side of the river. When the waters receded, they left behind nutrient-rich silt that made the soil more fertile. Since 1970, the Aswan High Dam has reduced the Nile's flooding, and today's farmers have to use fertilizers on their fields.

Flooded farmhouses in
Machland, Austria, August 2002

INLAND FLOODING
In 2002, after torrential rain in central Europe, the Danube, Elbe, and Vltava rivers flooded. Flood defenses failed and vast areas of the Czech Republic, Austria, and Germany were under water. In the Czech capital, Prague, floodwaters filled the underground railway system and severely damaged historic buildings. When rivers burst their banks in urban areas, floodwaters can turn towns into vast lakes, or rush down hills in flash floods.

Map showing the annual amount
of rainfall around the world

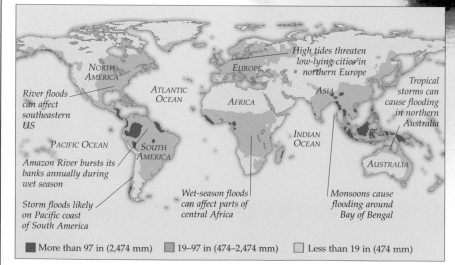

River floods can affect southeastern US

High tides threaten low-lying cities in northern Europe

NORTH AMERICA

ATLANTIC OCEAN

EUROPE

ASIA

AFRICA

Tropical storms can cause flooding in northern Australia

PACIFIC OCEAN

SOUTH AMERICA

INDIAN OCEAN

Amazon River bursts its banks annually during wet season

Storm floods likely on Pacific coast of South America

Wet-season floods can affect parts of central Africa

Monsoons cause flooding around Bay of Bengal

AUSTRALIA

■ More than 97 in (2,474 mm) ■ 19–97 in (474–2,474 mm) □ Less than 19 in (474 mm)

THE WORLD'S RAINFALL
The average rainfall across the world is 40 in (1,000 mm) per year. But this is not evenly distributed. Many parts of the world have moderate rainfall, while others suffer droughts and some are regularly under water. The amount of rain a region receives depends on many factors, including air temperature, the shape and size of the land mass, and season.

MELTING GLACIER
The gradual melting of frozen river ice or mountain glaciers is often so slow that it cannot cause a flood. Sometimes, as the ice begins to break up, floating chunks can pile up to form a dam across the river, causing the river to overflow upstream. When the ice dam cracks or bursts, the buildup of water is released downstream in an icy flash flood.

Pond formed by melted ice (meltwater)

DIVERTING THE WATERS
Along some rivers, engineers have built water channels called sluices to direct water away from flood-prone areas. River levels are monitored constantly, since even slight rises upstream (near the river's source) may lead to a flood downstream (near the sea). When the sluice gates are opened, the excess water gushes through into a runoff lake.

Sluice gates on Three Gorges Dam, Hubei Province, China

PROTECTING LONDON
London's Thames Barrier protects the city from flooding caused by the tidal Thames River. The barrier's gates close to prevent tidal surges from traveling upriver into the city. Tidal rivers such as the Thames are at risk from floods due to unusually high tides, and storm surges.

Gates open to allow river traffic through

Doppler radar dome receives returning radio waves

Red areas show approaching storm

Color codes for storm magnitude

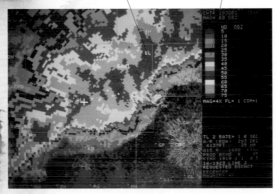

SEVERE WEATHER WARNINGS
Today, it is possible to make accurate weather forecasts using Doppler radar equipment. The system locates storms and measures their speed and direction by bouncing radio waves off clouds. This weather map, made from a Doppler radar readout, shows a severe thunderstorm in Kansas.

Raging waters

WHEN A FLOOD STRIKES, roads become impassable, either too deep in water for vehicles to travel, or washed away by the floodwaters. With no way to escape the flood, people climb higher and higher as the waters rise, first to the upper stories of buildings, then onto roofs or into high trees. There, they wait for rescuers to arrive in boats or helicopters. One way to protect people from the danger of flooding would be to stop building homes on flood plains. But many large cities already exist on flood plains. In heavily populated, low-lying countries, such as Bangladesh and the Netherlands, there is not enough higher ground.

Ball of smoking incense

NOAH'S ARK
In the Bible story, Noah's ark floated on a flood caused by 40 days of heavy rain. Noah and his passengers stayed on the ark for a year until the floodwaters dried up.

THE RIGHT RAIN
In ancient times, as today, rain was vital to water crops, but storms could destroy them—and wreck villages. The Mayan people made offerings to Chac, their god of rain, in the hope that he would provide rain but keep floods at bay.

The usual course of the Yangtze River

CONTROLLING THE YANGTZE RIVER
The banks of China's Yangtze River burst regularly after heavy rain, killing thousands of people in some years. One of the worst floods occurred in August 2002, when some 900,000 people were displaced. Ten years earlier, the Chinese government had begun work on the Three Gorges Dam (the world's largest dam), designed to control the flooding. It is due to be finished in 2009, but its construction may have unintended side effects, such as triggering local earth tremors.

Houses under 3 ft (1 m) of water

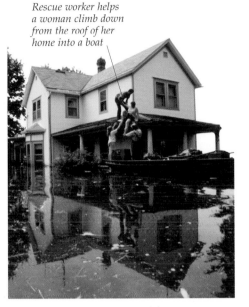

ESCAPING THE WATER
As the waters of the Mississippi and its tributaries rose in 1993, people climbed onto roofs and into trees to escape the rising floodwater. Forty-five people died in the floods and 70,000 were left homeless.

Rescue worker helps a woman climb down from the roof of her home into a boat

ROAD TO NOWHERE
This collapsed bridge in Quincy, Illinois, became submerged when the largest US river, the Mississippi, and its tributary the Missouri, flooded in 1993. An area over 31,000 sq miles (80,000 sq km) was under water. The devastating floods occurred when dams and levees burst following ten times the usual amount of spring rainfall on the central plains.

Stranded passengers await rescue on the bus's roof

788 ROYAL EAGLE

FLASH FLOODS
Typhoon Winnie hit the Philippines in November 2004, bringing with it enough rain to create flash floods and landslides. Two buses traveling in a region north of the capital, Manila, were almost swept away by the flood. Passengers climbed onto the roofs of the vehicles to escape the raging waters.

Container for emergency food ration

LIVING WITH FLOODS
Bangladeshi women and children line up, waist-deep in floodwater, for emergency supplies. Low-lying Bangladesh lies between two huge rivers, the Ganges and the Brahmaputra, and its people are accustomed to flooding every year during the monsoon. But in 1997–98, the weather pattern called El Niño triggered such a huge increase in the monsoon rain that two-thirds of the country was inundated. Ten million people lost their homes.

Drought and famine

It is hard to tell exactly when a drought starts. When there is much less rain than usual, the soil gradually dries out and plants begin to die. When water levels drop and cracks appear in dry lakes and river beds, the drought is well under way. If it continues, the drought may cause a famine and people and animals starve. The best preparation for drought is to store water in reservoirs or tanks when there is plenty, but the driest places never have enough water. In such places, drought cannot be prevented, but the famine that often follows can, providing that water supplies, food resources, and aid are supplied before people begin to suffer.

VANISHING SEA
The Aral Sea between Kazakhstan and Uzbekistan is half the size it once was. Since the 1960s, much of the water from rivers that feed into the Aral Sea has been diverted for irrigation. The shrinking sea has become far more salty, too, killing the fish that once provided 3 percent of the Soviet Union's total catch.

Boat grounded on sands that were once under the Aral Sea

UNDERGROUND WATER
In 2003, Gujarat, India, suffered its worst drought in ten years. The only water left was to be found in deep wells such as this one. People had to travel long distances, often on foot, and wait their turn for just a few pots of water. When drought dries up the soil and surface water, groundwater still flows deep under the ground, trapped by hard layers of rock. Deep wells tap into this resource.

Field of dried-out sunflowers in Spain

THIRSTY CROPS
In a drought, the first people to suffer are often farmers, when crops such as these sunflowers die. In wealthy countries, other people may be affected when water shortages lead to watering bans. However, there is usually enough water stored in reservoirs for drinking and washing until rain replenishes water supplies.

HOLDING BACK THE DESERT
Rainfall is unpredictable on the fringes of deserts, such as in Niger on the edge of the Sahara Desert. During droughts, the sand dunes can spread, burying surrounding towns and farms. To help stop this, farmers plant crops such as millet in the dunes, which binds the sand together and stops it from blowing toward the fields.

Burial mounds

DUST BOWL

During the 1930s, a severe drought hit the Great Plains of the US. Intensive farming had robbed the soil of nutrients and, when drought struck, the soil turned to dust and blew away. The region became known as the Dust Bowl. Crop failures and famine soon followed the drought and, by 1937, half a million people had abandoned their farms.

Brick lining stops soil from collapsing into the well

Metal pots lowered on ropes to reach groundwater

Animal carcass, a common sight during severe droughts

FAMINE

When drought hit the African countries of Sudan and Ethiopia in 1984–85, first crops failed and then livestock began to starve. With neither crops nor livestock, the people had no food and no income to buy any, and they too began to starve. In the severe famine that followed, 450,000 people in the region died.

REFUGEE CAMP

In the worst droughts, people leave their stricken land to gather in refugee camps. Here they can receive water, food, and shelter until the drought lifts and they can return to their homes. Governments, or aid organizations such as Doctors Without Borders and Oxfam, supply clean water, food, medicines, and shelters to the camps.

Wildfire

Forest fire warning

F**ROM THE FIRST FLICKER** of flame in dry grass, a wildfire spreads rapidly across the countryside. Flames leap from tree to tree and burning embers fly around in the wind, igniting more vegetation, while terrified animals flee from the oncoming flames. Also known as forest fires or brush fires, wildfires are a regular occurrence during the long, dry summers in the forests of California, southern Europe, and Australia. Today, wildfires are sometimes left to burn themselves out and the landscape to regenerate naturally. However, when a wildfire gets out of control, firefighters battle to stop the fire from destroying whole wildernesses or burning down houses.

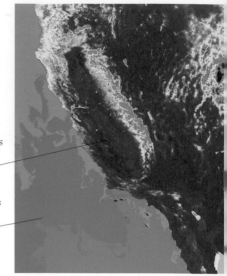

Dark red areas are the hottest, showing ground temperatures above 130°F (55°C)

Cool blue-green area is the Pacific Ocean

HEATWAVE
This thermal satellite image shows ground temperatures in California during a heatwave in May 2004. The heatwave led to an early start to the wildfire season. Wildfires are worst in very hot years when lack of rain dries out the vegetation, providing easily-ignited fuel for the fires.

LIGHTNING BOLT
About half of all wildfires are started by people, either deliberately or accidentally; the rest start naturally. The spark that lights most natural wildfires is a bolt of lightning during a summer storm. Dry vegetation provides the fuel a fire needs, and storm winds fan the flames. In minutes, a landscape can be transformed.

Thick, choking smoke rises from a land-clearance fire

YELLOWSTONE FIRE
In 1988, a very dry summer and exceptionally strong winds caused a season of major wildfires at Yellowstone National Park. Throughout August, fires burned continuously. In one single day, 150,000 acres (60,700 hectares) of woodland were consumed. The Park had to suspend its natural fire policy of leaving wildfires to burn themselves out. Firefighters and military recruits were brought in from all over the country to combat the flames.

Rising heat sucks in air at the bottom, fueling the fire with oxygen

FARMERS' FIRES
In the rainforests of Southeast Asia and South America, farmers clear land by burning down trees and undergrowth. They grow crops on the land for a few years, and then leave it to become forest again. But farmers' fires are difficult to control, and they sometimes grow into dangerous wildfires.

NEW GROWTH

Wildfires are a vital part of the life cycle of these North American lodgepole pines. These trees release their seeds only in the intense heat of a fire. Forest fires can be beneficial to other plants and trees, too. They clear the forest floor for new seedlings to grow, return nutrients to the soil, and kill off pests and diseases.

FIGHTING FIRES

Firefighters use various methods to tackle wildfires. They spray water or chemicals onto the burning vegetation to lower its temperature and make the fuel less flammable. They may cut down or burn vegetation around the area where the fire is heading so that the fire runs out of fuel. Firefighters may also use bulldozers to create wide, bare trenches that the flames cannot leap over.

Flames, fanned by winds of 55 mph (90 km/h), are capable of leaping over the highway to reach trees on the other side

Fighting fires

FIRE ENGINE
In urban areas, fire engines can connect their hoses to fire hydrants for water to douse the flames. In the wilderness, firefighters drive tanks of water to the scene of the fire, or pump it from nearby water sources.

IT MAY TAKE more than a week for firefighters, working on the ground and in the air, to bring a major wildfire under control. In the most remote regions, firefighters may have to battle their way to the heart of the fire through leaping flames, falling trees, choking smoke, and 930°F (500°C) temperatures. But some wildfires are unstoppable. In 1997, after months of drought, more than 100 fires were blazing among the rainforests of Indonesia. Firefighting experts flew in from around the world, but many fires could not be brought under control. At last, the long-awaited monsoon rains fell, extinguishing the flames until the next year's wildfire season.

Cruise speed is 126 mph (203 km/h)

Helicopter carries one pilot, two fire captains, and eight firefighters

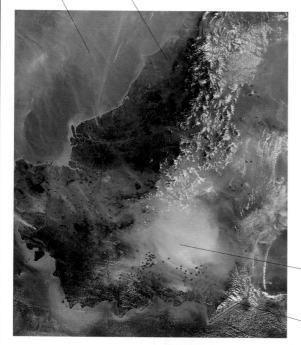

Indian Ocean

Island of Borneo

AN ISLAND BURNS
Throughout the summer of 2002, glowing fires and a blanket of smoke across Borneo, southeast Asia, were clearly visible from space. Logging companies started the fires deliberately to clear parts of the rainforest, but they rapidly got out of hand. The fires, which also struck the nearby island of Sumatra, destroyed an area of forest half the size of Switzerland. Even after a rainforest fire has been put out, the layer of peat under the forest continues to smolder and can reignite the flames.

Smoke from wildfires

Red dots show fires still burning

CHOKING SMOG
Raging fires consumed over 750,000 acres (300,000 hectares) of forest in Southeast Asia in 1997. The smoke created a gray haze of choking smog that affected more than 70 million people. In some areas, one day's exposure to the polluted air was equivalent to smoking dozens of cigarettes. Protective masks were worn by many people in an attempt to minimize damage to their lungs.

Health worker hands masks to a commuter

Sparks shoot out as the tree ignites

FLAMING TREE
Australian eucalyptus trees are rich in natural oils, which prevent them from drying out in the arid climate. But it makes them very flammable. In the hot, dry Australian summer, the intense heat of an approaching fire can cause the trees to spontaneously ignite. When the fire is over, new growth can spring from beneath the charred bark, and the eucalyptus' fire-resistant seeds soon germinate in the ash-rich soil.

Tank can hold 350 gallons (1,360 liters) of water or foam

Brightly colored, fire-resistant clothing

FIGHTING BUSHFIRES
In 2002, wildfires reached the fringes of urban areas in New South Wales, Australia. Firefighters struggled to turn back the flames, but 170 homes were destroyed. Around the Australian bush, firefighters are now carrying out regular, controlled burns to clear the dry undergrowth. This helps to prevent major fires.

High collar protects neck from branches during jump

Water turned to steam by the heat of the flames

SMOKEJUMPERS
In remote areas, firefighters known as smokejumpers parachute in to tackle small fires before they can spread. Smokejumpers cannot parachute with much equipment, so pumps and heavy tools are dropped separately. When the job is done, the smokejumpers often have to hike out of the area carrying all the equipment with them.

DOUSING THE FLAMES
Wildfires are an annual hazard to people living near forested areas of southern California. In 2004 alone, over 5,500 fires spread across 168,000 acres (68,000 hectares) of the state, destroying more than 1,000 buildings. The California fire service has specially adapted helicopters that can scoop or suck up water from a nearby water source, such as a lake. The load is dumped onto the hottest part of the fire or onto surrounding vegetation to make it less likely to catch fire.

Helmet with heavy mesh face mask

Gear bag

Climate change

Over millions of years, Earth's climate has swung from freezing ice ages to swelteringly hot periods many times. Long-term climate change is caused by variations in the Sun's heat output, in the tilt of Earth, and in the distance between Earth and Sun as the two move through space. For about the last 100 years, our planet has been growing warmer, but in the last few decades, the rate of change has increased dramatically. Many scientists believe that this global warming is largely due to the enormous volumes of polluting gases released by burning fossil fuels. Some scientists predict that global warming will bring more extreme weather, with fiercer storms and deadlier droughts.

Sunspot

Solar flare

SOLAR ACTIVITY
The amount of heat given out by the Sun varies over time. When it increases, there are more sunspots and solar flares on the Sun's surface. In the 1990s, increased solar activity reduced cloud cover over Earth in some years so that more of the Sun's heat reached the planet's surface. This helped raise global temperatures slightly during those years.

Russia

Greenland

NORTH POLE

ARCTIC SEA ICE, 1979
One of the clearest effects of global warming is the reduced extent of sea ice (frozen sea water) in the Arctic. This satellite image shows the extent of the Arctic sea ice in 1979, around the North Pole. An ice sheet covers much of the eastern coast of Greenland, and sea ice stretches as far as the northern coast of Russia.

ARCTIC SEA ICE, 2003
This satellite image clearly shows how much the Arctic ice sheet had shrunk by 2003. Scientists estimate that some ice sheets have melted by 15 percent in this 25-year period. If temperatures keep rising, the ocean's water will expand slightly as it warms and water melting off the land will add to the sea's volume. Sea levels will rise enough to flood low-lying coasts.

POLAR HABITAT UNDER THREAT
Reduction in the sea ice threatens the survival of polar bears, because they spend much of their lives traveling across the ice, hunting for seals in the Arctic waters. Warmer conditions in the Arctic may mean that much of the floating ice sheet will become a seasonal feature, melting in summer and reforming in winter. As the temperature rises, massive cracks appear in the polar ice sheet. Gradually, chunks of ice break off and float away.

Drifting chunks of ice melt faster than the solid ice sheet

Spring in the Northern
Hemisphere and fall in the
Southern Hemisphere

Earth's orbit changes shape over
thousands of years, varying between
a circle and an ellipse (oval)

Northern Hemisphere
tilted away from the
Sun, so it is winter here

23.5° current
angle of tilt

Earth's axis

Direction of
Earth's spin

Vertical line
through
Earth

SUN
(not to scale)

Fall in the Northern
Hemisphere and spring in
the Southern Hemisphere

Northern Hemisphere
tilted toward the Sun,
so it is summer here

Earth orbits (travels all the
way around) the Sun every
365.2 days, or roughly once a year

TILT OF EARTH
The seasons are created by
the tilt of Earth toward the
Sun, with regions nearest
the Sun receiving more heat.
This angle of tilt changes
slightly over thousands of
years. The greater the tilt,
the greater the difference
between the seasons.
Sometimes this fluctuation
coincides with changes in
Earth's orbit, which take the
planet farther from or closer
to the Sun. Then Earth's
temperature can vary enough
to produce an ice age or to
raise global temperatures
several degrees.

BLEACHED CORAL
When coral dies, it loses all its vibrant
color, like this ghostly white patch on
a Pacific Ocean reef. Microscopic
algae (simple plants) live as
partners within some corals,
and are essential for the coral's
survival. But increases as
small as 1.8°F (1°C) in the
temperature of the shallow
seas can kill this algae.

Bleached coral
has no algae

Undamaged coral

LEARNING FROM THE PAST
Geologists drill samples called cores from the
ancient ice deep inside the Antarctic ice sheet.
The ice cores reveal information about surface
temperature over thousands of years, as the ice
sheet developed. Ice cores can also show how much
carbon dioxide, volcanic ash, dust, and pollen used
to exist in the atmosphere. Studying how climate
and atmosphere have changed in the past may help
scientists predict how it will change in the future.

Hollow drill pipe for
extracting ice core

Unnatural disasters

SOME DISASTERS are caused not by the natural world, but by its exploitation. Waste fumes from vehicles and from industry pollute the air we breathe. Burning fossil fuels (coal, oil, and gas) provides us with power, but it also releases gases into the atmosphere that speed up the natural rate of climate change. Supplies of these fuels are dwindling fast, but the amount of power we use continues to increase. Forests are being cut down for lumber and for farmland, and the oceans are being emptied of fish to provide us with food. Scientists warn that we urgently need to change the way we treat our planet. Cutting our use of natural resources and our production of pollution requires the agreement of the world's governments and action by ordinary people.

Pollution monitor

Dark blue area indicates reduced ozone above Antarctica

THINNING OZONE
High up in the atmosphere is a layer of a gas called ozone. Ozone, which forms when oxygen reacts with sunlight, blocks some of the Sun's harmful radiation. This radiation can cause skin cancer and other conditions. Gases called CFCs, used in refrigerators and aerosol sprays, react with oxygen and thin the ozone layer. This reduces the layer's ability to block the Sun's harmful rays. CFCs are now banned in many countries.

Redwood forest, northern California

POISONING THE AIR
Like many of the world's big cities, on hot days Santiago, Chile, is shrouded in a choking cloud of smog. This smog is a sooty fog containing a mixture of harmful gases, including carbon monoxide, produced when vehicle exhaust fumes react with sunlight. The polluted air can aggravate conditions such as asthma and bronchitis and cause eye irritations.

DEFORESTATION
Today, forests are being cut down faster than they are being replaced. Their trees provide lumber and, cleared of trees, the land can be used for farms and homes. But forests are vital to life on Earth. As part of the process called photosynthesis, trees absorb carbon dioxide and produce oxygen for animals to breathe. Deforestation can lead to the extinction of plants and animals by destroying their wild habitats.

In China, people flee a dust storm in a region suffering desertification

DESERTIFICATION
On the edges of deserts, years can go by with little or no rainfall. When these areas are heavily populated, the vegetation is stripped away, usually for animal feed, faster than it can regrow. Soon, desertification, the spread of desert conditions, sets in and the soil turns to barren dust. Along the edges of Asian and African deserts, millions of the world's poorest people are losing their land and their livelihoods as the deserts spread.

Catch of herring on a Norwegian trawler

Gray areas show coral damaged by dynamite

DWINDLING RESOURCES
Factory trawlers like this can catch and process several hundred tons of fish a day. Fish account for 10 percent of the protein eaten by humans worldwide and, as the world population grows, the demand for fish grows, too. Fish stocks are falling rapidly around the world and some species face extinction.

Cutting down a large area of trees can be very harmful to wildlife

BLAST FISHING
Among the world's most beautiful and productive environments, coral reefs are being damaged by an extraordinarily destructive form of fishing—blasting fish out of the water with dynamite. In parts of the developing world, blast fishing is used as a cheap, quick way to harvest fish, but it kills the coral beneath the shallow waters. It can take more than 20 years before the coral begins to recover.

ACID RAIN
These lifeless trees may look as if they have been hit by drought, but in fact, acid rain has killed them. Burning fossil fuels releases nitrogen and sulfur oxides, which form acids in the atmosphere. The wind carries these acids far from the cities and industries that produce them, until they fall as acid rain, killing trees and poisoning rivers.

Infectious diseases

THE DEADLIEST DISASTERS are not due to wild weather or the movements of Earth. They are caused by organisms so tiny that they can be seen only under powerful microscopes. Infectious diseases, including malaria, cholera, tuberculosis, and AIDS, are responsible for more than 13 million premature deaths throughout the world each year. These diseases are caused by bacteria, fungi, viruses, and other microorganisms, which invade the body through cuts, via insect bites, through our mouths and noses as we breathe, and in the food and drinks we consume. Some can even kill by destroying the crops we depend on for food.

Piercing-sucking mouthparts adapted to feed on blood

DEADLY FLEA
In the 14th century, bubonic plague struck Asia and Europe, killing 40 million people. The Black Death, as it was known, was spread by the black rats that swarmed the streets. The rats were hosts for the carriers—fleas. When an infected flea bit a human, its saliva transmitted the bacteria that causes plague.

Long hind legs for jumping from host to host

INFECTIOUS DROPLETS
Disease-carrying organisms can be spread in droplets of water that explode from the mouth or nose in a sneeze. The relatively harmless common cold is spread this way, but so are much more serious diseases, such as smallpox and tuberculosis.

Air rushes from the lungs at 95 mph (150 km/h)

Rwandan refugees skim a mud puddle for their drinking water

POWER OF THE MICROSCOPE
Scientists can identify and study the microorganisms that cause disease using microscopes. This scanning electron microscope can magnify up to 250,000 times. It works by bouncing a beam of electrons off a sample to create a black and white 3-D image—color is added by a computer. Dutch scientist Anton van Leeuwenhoek (1632–1723) was the first person to observe tiny living organisms such as bacteria and blood cells under a microscope.

DIRTY WATER
In the aftermath of wars and natural disasters, when refugees are gathered in temporary camps with limited supplies of clean water, one of the biggest threats to health is an outbreak of cholera. This deadly infection is caused by bacteria that thrive in dirty water. It causes acute diarrhea and vomiting, which can quickly lead to severe dehydration.

POTATO BLIGHT

This picture, produced by a scanning electron microscope, shows a tiny fungus, called *Phytophthora infestans*. Fungi are tiny plantlike organisms that feed on dead or living plants and animals. *Phytophthora infestans* causes potato blight, which rots the vegetable. Potato blight decimated the potato crop across Europe in the 1840s, and led to starvation and death for a million people in Ireland, where potatoes were the major food crop.

Potato blight mold spot

Viewing port, for observing sample

Protein coat locks on to host cell, allowing it to be invaded

VIRUSES

This scanning electron micrograph shows the variola virus that causes smallpox. Much smaller than a bacterium, a virus is a tiny package of genetic material surrounded by a protein shell. Viruses cause diseases—from smallpox and AIDS to the common cold—by invading a host's cells with the protein on their shells, then injecting their own genetic material into the cells.

The virus's instructions for copying itself are contained in its DNA

Pressure-resistant shell encloses a vacuum chamber in which electrons bombard the sample

SMALLPOX SCARRING

This Nigerian wooden statue of the Spirit of Smallpox is covered in spots that represent the smallpox rash. Smallpox is no longer a threat, but it was a highly infectious disease that left victims covered in unsightly scars—if they were lucky enough to survive. There was no treatment for smallpox once it was contracted.

Epidemic

An outbreak of a disease that spreads rapidly through the population is known as an epidemic. When it begins to affect vast numbers of people over a wide area, it becomes pandemic. Today, the global AIDS pandemic is perhaps the most serious health threat facing the world. Some epidemics can be prevented by killing the disease-carrying organisms, such as mosquitoes and the deadly MRSA bacteria. Epidemics of diseases such as measles and smallpox can be avoided by vaccination. Health education can help prevent the spread of infections such as AIDS. Outbreaks of cholera and other waterborne diseases can be halted, before they become epidemics, as long as people live in sanitary conditions and have access to clean water.

Names of victims of the flu pandemic

FLU RESEARCH
These sample blocks contain lung and brain tissue from victims of the 1918–20 influenza (flu) pandemic, which killed 20 million people worldwide. Researchers hope to isolate the flu virus from the samples to discover why this strain of flu was so deadly. Flu viruses are difficult to treat because they can mutate into different forms.

VACCINATING THE WORLD
After smallpox caused two million deaths in 1967, the World Health Authority began a mass vaccination program in an attempt to eliminate the disease. A vaccination is a weak or dead form of the disease-causing organism which, injected into the body, stimulates the immune system to build up a resistance. Health workers traveled to the remote places of the world and carried out house-to-house searches to reach everyone who was at risk. The strategy was eventually successful and, in 1980, smallpox became the only major infectious human disease to be completely eradicated.

PLAGUE OUTBREAK
When pneumonic plague killed 51 people in Surat, western India, in 1994, hundreds of thousands of people fled in terror. Garbage was cleared from the streets and burned to destroy the disease-carrying rats. Pneumonic plague infects the lungs, but is caused by the same bacteria as the glandular disease bubonic plague, which swept Europe in the 1300s.

Multi-shot inoculation gun forces vaccine through the skin at high pressure, without a needle

CONTROLLING MALARIA

On the tiny island of Car Nicobar in the Bay of Bengal, an aid worker sprays stagnant water with chemicals to kill mosquito larvae. The 2004 Asian tsunami left behind a lot of stagnant water, creating breeding grounds for mosquitoes that could cause malaria outbreaks.

MOSQUITO LARVAE

Mosquito eggs hatch into larvae in water, and then develop into winged adults. The adult females feed on the blood of mammals, spreading diseases including malaria and dengue fever. Scientists have not yet found a way to prevent mosquitoes from breeding, so the mosquito larvae are killed to help prevent the spread of these diseases.

INFECTION CONTROL

Hygiene is one of the most important weapons in the fight against potentially lethal microorganisms, which thrive in dirty conditions. Some of these, such as MRSA, have developed a resistance to most antibiotics, so treating them is very difficult.

Disposable gloves, to help prevent spreading infection

HOSPITAL INFECTION

When MRSA (methicillin-resistant *Staphylococcus aureus*) bacteria are passed on to a hospital patient through a wound or a dirty medical tube, they can cause a severe infection. Patients found to be carrying MRSA are isolated to prevent the infection from spreading. They are treated with powerful antibiotics, but in the weakest patients, MRSA can be fatal.

MRSA bacteria

HIV, colored red, invades a blood cell

HIV AND AIDS

The Human Immunodeficiency Virus (HIV), which causes AIDS (Acquired Immune Deficiency Syndrome), kills white blood cells, multiplies, and spreads. As more and more blood cells are destroyed, the body loses the ability to fight off infections. Forty-two million people worldwide are infected with HIV, and AIDS is fast becoming one of the biggest killers in history.

White blood cell, colored green in this image

AIDS EDUCATORS

World AIDS Day is commemorated by lighting candles for victims of the disease. Campaigners around the world are trying to educate people about AIDS to help prevent its spread. There is no cure for AIDS, and many people in the developing world do not have access to the drugs that can slow the disease.

Future disasters

AS THE PLANET becomes more heavily populated, disasters such as volcanoes and tsunamis are more likely to cause catastrophic loss of life. The area affected by disasters may also be much greater—scientists expect a huge volcanic eruption in the US, and a megatsunami from the Canary Islands, although they hope these are a long way in the future. In our lifetimes, disaster is more likely to strike in the form of a new global pandemic, which could wipe out millions. There is one disaster capable of destroying all life on Earth in a single blow: a Near Earth Object (NEO) such as a huge meteorite or comet crashing into our planet.

SUPERVOLCANO
Below Yellowstone Park, a massive magma chamber heats the water that bursts from the famous geysers. If enough pressure built up in the magma chamber, it could cause the biggest volcanic eruption in recorded history, destroying much of the US and blasting enough ash into the air to cool Earth. Some scientists warn that an eruption at Yellowstone is now overdue.

KILLER FLU
When diseases develop strains capable of infecting more than one species, they can become very potent. Avian influenza (bird flu) usually affects only poultry, but in Hong Kong in 1997 it began infecting humans. Health experts fear that the virus could become a global flu pandemic, killing more than 50 million people.

Mount Vesuvius

DEVASTATION OF ITALY
If Italy's Mount Vesuvius exploded in a massive volcanic eruption today, the effect would be far more devastating than when the volcano destroyed Pompeii in 79 ad. Southern Italy is now the most densely populated high-risk volcanic area on Earth. Six towns along the volcano's southern flank would be in danger, including the city of Naples, which has a population of one million people.

RACE AGAINST TIME
After outbreaks of bird flu in China, poultry workers wore masks and gloves to stop possible contamination. At present, the virus can be spread only by direct contact with birds, but experts say it is only a matter of time before person-to-person infection develops. Then the disease could spread worldwide, carried between countries by travelers before they even realize they are infected. Medical researchers are still searching for a vaccine.

MEGATSUNAMI
Some scientists calculate that a volcanic eruption could send the western half of the island of La Palma, one of Spain's Canary Islands, crashing into the sea. The 500-billion-ton landslide would send a megatsunami racing across the Atlantic to engulf the east coast of the United States, from New York to Miami, with waves 65 ft (20 m) high.

Influenza virus particles shown in red

Culture cells used in virus research shown in blue

First 4-ft (1.2-m) reflecting telescope

Second 4-ft (1.2-m) reflecting telescope

The Cumbre Vieja ridge could collapse into the sea

Assembly rotates on its base, enabling the two telescopes to track objects

TRACKING THE SKIES
Optical telescopes, such as this twin telescope at Maui Observatory in Hawaii, can track the movement of Near Earth Objects (NEOs) that could collide with Earth. NASA currently keeps track of 1,855 NEOs—none of them are heading for Earth just yet. The impact of an object 0.6 miles (1 km) wide would destroy everything within 300 miles (500 km).

Artist's impression of the meteorite strike that destroyed the dinosaurs

COLLISION COURSE
Powerful evidence suggests that, 65 million years ago, a huge object 6 miles (10 km) wide hit Mexico's Yucatan Peninsula. The impact produced a megatsunami, with waves 0.6 miles (1 km) high. A cloud of water vapor and dust rose high into the atmosphere, blocking out the Sun and creating a global winter that lasted many months. It is thought that this single event brought about the extinction of the dinosaurs and two-thirds of other animal species. To protect the Earth from any Near Earth Object (NEO) that might threaten disaster on a similar scale, scientists are searching for a way to destroy these objects with nuclear warheads, or push them off course by firing missiles at them.

Did you know?

AMAZING FACTS

So many volcanoes occur around the rim of the Pacific Plate that this zone is known as the "Ring of Fire."

In 1902, Meteor Crater, Arizona, was the first crater on Earth to be recognized as being created by a meteorite impact. Before this, people thought the feature was the remains of an ancient volcano.

Forest fires clear trees and shrubs from the ground. Fresh seedlings of California's giant sequoias flourish after the fire because they now have the space and access to sunlight they need to grow. The mature sequoia's thick, spongy bark protects the living part of the trunk from burning, and its deep roots reach water far underground. No wonder some of these trees live to be more than 3,000 years old.

Burned giant sequoia, California

Rain may fall only once every eight years in parts of the Sahara Desert.

About 150,000 noticeable earthquakes happen every year. More than a million are detected by seismograms.

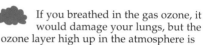

Rain darkens the desert sands

Scientists used to call tsunamis "seismic sea waves" because they thought these waves were caused only by earthquakes. But these waves can also be caused by impacts on the water surface, so the name "tsunami," or "harbor wave," is now used.

If lightning strikes a tree, the moisture inside may boil, blowing the tree to pieces.

Thunder is the sound of air around a bolt of lightning exploding as it is heated to 54,000°F (30,000°C) in less than a second.

For a hurricane to develop over the sea, the sea temperature must be no lower than 80°F (27°C).

In January 1975, a tornado in McComb, Mississippi, threw three buses over a 7-ft- (2-m-) high wall.

In December 1952, 4,000 people died in smog in London, caused largely by burning coal as a heating fuel.

From 1550 to 1850, there were fewer solar flares or sunspots on the Sun than usual, which showed that the Sun emitted slightly less heat. This coincided with a cooler period in Earth's history known as the "Little Ice Age."

The 2004 tsunami washed away centuries of sand from the ruins of a 1,200-year-old lost city in Mahabalipuram, southern India.

The size of the seasonal "hole" in the ozone layer over Antarctica peaked at 11.3 million square miles (29.2 million square km) in 2002. The hole is gradually getting smaller, and may disappear by 2050.

Drought conditions vary from place to place, depending on how much rain is normal for the place and the season. In the US, a drought is declared after 21 days with less than 30 percent of normal rainfall. In the Sahara Desert, there have to be two years without rain before a drought is declared.

If you are caught out in the open when a tornado strikes, lie down flat on the ground in a hollow or low-lying area with your hands over your head, until it passes.

The oldest rocks on land are about 3.5 billion years old, but the oldest rocks on the ocean floor are about 200 million years old, because the new sea floor is being added where plates pull apart, while old sea floor is being subducted elsewhere.

If you breathed in the gas ozone, it would damage your lungs, but the ozone layer high up in the atmosphere is vital to screen out harmful radiation.

More earthquakes happen in the Northern Hemisphere than in the Southern Hemisphere.

When the Xiangjiang River in China flooded in August 2002, some residents of the city of Changsha had to move out of their flooded homes to live on a staircase leading to a bridge. The only way people could move around the city was by boat.

Flooding in Changsha, China

On December 26, 2004, a 10-year-old British girl noticed the water receding at Maikhao Beach, Phuket, Thailand. She had learned about tsunamis in geography class, and realized that a tsunami was about to happen. With the help of her parents, she warned people to leave the beach, and the evacuation saved 100 lives.

Fourteenth-century doctors had no idea how to cure the plague. Some doctors put dried toads on the patient's buboes (swellings) to draw out the poison. Others tried to burn the buboes away with red-hot irons.

QUESTIONS AND ANSWERS

Q How far can lightning travel?

A Lightning can travel over 6 miles (10 km). Even if a storm is not directly overhead, you could still get struck by lightning.

Q How are hurricane names decided?

A Hurricanes are given a name from a list drawn up several years in advance. Each new hurricane begins with the next letter of the alphabet; male and female names alternate. After a devastating hurricane happens, its name is retired.

Searching for avalanche survivors in Switzerland, 2002

Q How are avalanche survivors found?

A After an avalanche, teams of rescue workers move across the soft, fallen snow, gently probing with long sticks. If the stick meets an obstruction, the rescuers dig in that spot to see if someone if buried there. Some skiers carry electronic devices that signal their position to rescuers if an avalanche strikes.

Q What is smog?

A Smog is a mixture of smoke and fog. It is worst when pollutants accumulate in a shallow layer of cold air trapped under a "lid" of warmer air. Cities situated in a bowl surrounded by hills, such as Los Angeles and Mexico City, are more prone to smog because low-level air is sheltered from winds and a warm-air lid can readily settle over it.

Q How did scientists figure out that the continents move around Earth?

A After noticing that the continent of South America looked as if it would fit against the western side of Africa, in 1915 German scientist Alfred Wegener stated that today's continents were once part of a single landmass. It took over thirty years before his theory was generally accepted.

Q Which infectious disease is becoming the biggest killer?

A AIDS has already killed 22 million people worldwide, and experts say by 2010 the death toll will be 65 million.

Q Is it possible to harness the energy of a volcano?

A In volcanically active countries such as Iceland and New Zealand, power stations pump water down into Earth's crust. The burning-hot magma turns the water into steam, which rises to turn turbines that generate electricity. This type of power is known as geothermal energy.

Q In which direction do tornadoes spin?

A Tornadoes in the Northern Hemisphere spin counterclockwise; in the Southern Hemisphere they spin clockwise.

Q Why is the weather pattern that switches the direction of warm water currents in the Pacific Ocean called El Niño?

A El Niño means "Christ Child" in Spanish. The weather pattern is named after a seasonal change in ocean currents off Peru that normally occurs around Christmas.

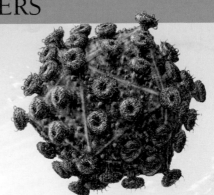

Particle of the HIV virus

Record-breakers

✸ **HEAVIEST HAILSTONE**
In 1986, huge hailstones weighing more than 2.2 lb (1 kg) fell in Gopalganj, Bangladesh.

✸ **MOST VOLCANOES**
Indonesia has more volcanoes than any other country, with 130 active volcanoes and another 270 that are either dormant or extinct.

✸ **MOST EXPENSIVE NATURAL DISASTER**
The costliest natural disaster to date is the Kobe earthquake, estimated at $130 billion.

✸ **WORST RECORDED LIGHTNING STRIKE**
In December 1963, lightning struck an aircraft over Maryland, which crashed, killing 81 people.

✸ **FASTEST AVALANCHE**
In 1980, the volcanic eruption of Mount St. Helens triggered the fastest recorded avalanche, reaching speeds of 250 mph (402 km/h).

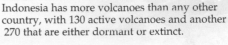

Storm waves caused by El Niño strike Malibu, CA, 1983

Timeline

THIS TIMELINE OUTLINES some of the most devastating natural disasters that have happened throughout the history of the world. From the earliest times, scientists and inventors have studied the causes of these disasters and attempted to predict them or to make their results less destructive. Some of the innovations and discoveries they have made are cataloged here, too.

Tyrannosaurus rex (65 MYA)

250 million years ago (MYA)
In the largest mass extinction in Earth's history, 90 percent of all living organisms die out. Scientists cannot find a single cause, but massive volcanic eruptions in Siberia may have altered the climate worldwide.

65 MYA
A massive meteorite hits the Yucatán Peninsula, Mexico, generating a megatsunami that wipes out 50 percent of all species, including the dinosaurs.

1.8 MYA to present day
Periodic fluctuations in Earth's climate lead to glacial periods known as ice ages, when much of Earth is covered in ice sheets, and warmer interglacial periods when the ice sheets retreat. Earth is currently in an interglacial period.

c. 2200 BC
Records suggest that the city of Troy, in modern Turkey, was hit by a meteorite shower that set fire to the city and killed the entire population.

c. 1640 BC
The island of Santorini in the Mediterranean erupts, causing a tsunami that destroys the Minoan civilization on Crete. Many people link this event with the legend of Atlantis.

340 BC
Greek philosopher Aristotle writes Meteorologica, a thesis on weather formation and patterns. His ideas are believed to be accurate for 2,000 years, when scientific investigations prove that many are wrong.

AD 79
In Italy, the eruption of Mount Vesuvius destroys the towns of Pompeii and Herculaneum.

AD 132
In China, Zhang Heng invents the first earthquake detector.

1348
Black Death, or bubonic plague, arrives in Europe from the east. It will kill 30 million Europeans—a quarter of Europe's population.

1441
Concerned about the lives of peasants working on the land, King Sejong of Korea orders the development of a rain gauge to forecast floods and droughts.

1492–1900
Ninety percent of the native American population dies, many as a result of infectious diseases, such as smallpox, introduced to the continent by Europeans.

1556
On January 3, the most destructive earthquake in recorded history hits Shaanxi province, China, killing 800,000 people. Many are buried alive.

Minoan palace at Knossos (1640 BC)

Black Death, London (1348)

1703
Edo (now Tokyo), Japan, is destroyed by an earthquake and tsunami that kill 200,000 people.

1752
Benjamin Franklin's dangerous experiments with electricity later lead to the invention of the lightning conductor.

Benjamin Franklin's lightning experiment, 1752

1755
Triggered by an earthquake, a tsunami hits Lisbon, Portugal, with waves 50 ft (15 m) high. About 60,000 people are killed in the disaster.

1792
A debris avalanche from the side of Mount Unzen near Nagasaki, Japan, creates a tsunami that kills more than 14,000.

1798
English doctor Edward Jenner develops the first-ever vaccine, against smallpox.

1815
Mount Tambora blows apart the island of Sumbawa, Indonesia, in the largest eruption in recorded history. The dust and gas produced affect the climate worldwide, and 1815 becomes known as the "year without a summer."

1840s
Potato blight destroys potato crops throughout Europe, bringing widespread famine. In Ireland, where most of the population relies on potatoes for food, more than one million die.

1846
Irish researcher Thomas R. Robinson invents the spinning cup anemometer to measure wind speed.

1851–66
China's Yellow and Yangtze Rivers flood repeatedly over the triangle of land between them known as the "Rice Bowl." Up to 50 million people drown in the 15 years of flooding.

1860s
Weather-observing stations are set up around the globe. Information collected over a wide area can be compared and will be used to make accurate weather forecasts.

1864
Inspired by Swiss philanthropist Henri Dunant, the International Committee of the Red Cross, the first international aid organization, is founded in Geneva, Switzerland.

1874–76
Measles kills a third of the native population of Fiji, Polynesia. The disease has been introduced to the island by Europeans.

1882–83
German scientist Robert Koch identifies the bacteria that cause cholera and tuberculosis.

1883
Eruption of the volcanic island of Krakatau, Indonesia, generates a tsunami that kills 36,000 people in Java and Sumatra.

1885
British geologist John Milne invents the first modern seismograph for measuring earth tremors.

1900
In the worst local natural disaster in the history of the US, a hurricane and storm surge kill more than 6,000 in Galveston, Texas.

1902
On May 8, Mount Pelée, Martinique, erupts, leaving only two survivors out of a population of 30,000 in the town of St. Pierre, and causing a tsunami in the Caribbean.

TransAmerica earthquake-proof skyscraper, 1972

Floods, England, 1953

1906
The Great San Francisco Earthquake is estimated to have killed nearly 3,000. The fires that follow burn the mostly wooden city to the ground. New buildings have to conform to earthquake safety regulations.

1908
A meteorite explodes before impact with the ground near Tunguska, in a remote region of northern Russia, in June. The blast flattens 850 sq miles (2,200 sq km) of forest, but no one dies in this largely unpopulated area.

1911
On January 31, on the island of Luzon in the Philippines, the Ta'al volcano obliterates 13 villages and towns. Most of the 1,335 victims choke on ash and sulfur dioxide.

1917–18
Influenza epidemic kills 20,000,000 people worldwide.

1921–22
A drought and civil war devastates the entire region of Volga, Russia, causing widespread famine. More than 20 million people are affected.

1923
The Great Kanto Earthquake hits Tokyo, Japan, killing more than 140,000 people and destroying 360,000 buildings.

1928
Scottish scientist Alexander Fleming discovers the antibiotic penicillin. Not until 1941 is the drug ready to use.

1930s
Droughts combined with poor farming methods lead to the creation of the "Dust Bowl" across the states of Kansas, Oklahoma, Texas, Colorado, and New Mexico. Famine drives 300,000 people to abandon their farms.

1931
After heavy rain, the Yangtze River in China rises to 95 ft (29 m) above its normal level, flooding large areas of China and destroying crops. In the floods and famine that follow, and estimated 3,700,000 people die.

1935
American Charles Richter invents the Richter scale to measure earthquake magnitude.

1946
Following a tsunami that struck Hawaii, the Pacific Tsunami Warning Center is set up in Honolulu.

1946
The United Nations International Children's Emergency Fund (UNICEF) is founded to provide emergency aid to children in case of war or natural disaster.

1948
The World Health Organization (WHO) is established by the United Nations. One of its aims is to support programs designed to eradicate diseases.

1953
A storm surge in the North Sea hits the Netherlands with 13-ft (4-m) waves, killing 1,800 people. It produces 8-ft (2.5-m) waves in Essex, England, where 300 people die.

1958
Lituya Bay, Alaska, is hit by the largest local tsunami in recent history, when a massive landslide produces a wave 1,720 ft (525 m) high.

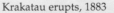

Krakatau erupts, 1883

1960
On April 1, the first weather satellite, TIROS-1, is sent into space from Cape Canaveral, FL.

1960
In May, the largest earthquake ever recorded, measuring 9.5 on the Richter scale, hits Chile, causing tsunamis that affect Chile, Peru, Hawaii, and Japan.

1968–74
A seven-year drought occurs in the Sahel region of Africa. By 1974, 50 million people are relying on food from international aid agencies.

1970
An earthquake measuring 7.7 occurs off the coast of Peru, causing massive avalanches and mudslides in the Nevados Huascarán mountains, which kill 18,000 people.

1971

The worst hurricane (tropical cyclone) in recent history hits Bangladesh with winds up to 155 mph (250 km/h) and a 25-ft (7.5-m) storm surge. The death toll ranges from 300,000 to one million people.

1976

On July 28, an earthquake measuring 7.8 hits Tangshan, China, where 93 percent of the city's mud-brick houses collapse, crushing 242,000 people to death.

1979

After a worldwide vaccination campaign, the WHO announces that smallpox is eradicated.

1980

On May 18, Mount St. Helens, WA, erupts. A successful evacuation is carried out, and only 57 lives are lost.

1984–5

An extended drought in Ethiopia and Sudan kills 450,000 people.

1985

On November 13, the eruption of Nevado del Ruiz, Colombia, causes a mudslide that covers the town of Armero with 130 ft (40 m) of mud, killing 22,800 people.

1985

An earthquake measuring 8.1 hits Mexico City, killing more than 8,000, and leaving 30,000 homeless.

1988

In Armenia, an earthquake measuring 6.9 causes newly built apartment blocks to collapse, killing 25,000.

1991

Mount Pinatubo, Philippines, erupts in June, ejecting so much debris into the atmosphere that global temperatures drop slightly for the next 15 months.

Pakistan earthquake, 2005

1992

In August, Hurricane Andrew strikes the Bahamas, Florida, and Louisiana, killing more than 65 people and causing damage estimated at $20 billion.

1992

In December, a tsunami with waves reaching 85 ft (26 m) crashes onto the coast of Flores, Indonesia, killing 2,000 and leaving 90,000 homeless.

1993

Summer flooding on the Mississippi and Missouri rivers causes $12 billion worth of damage.

1995

In Kobe, Japan, 5,500 die as buildings collapse in an earthquake of magnitude 7.2 on the Richter scale.

1997

Pyroclastic flows from the Soufrière Hills inundate Plymouth, capital of Montserrat.

1997

In September, wildfires in Indonesia destroy more than 750,000 acres (300,000 hectares) of forest and bush, creating a widespread polluting haze.

1998

Flooding in Bangladesh caused by the very strong 1997/1998 El Niño kills 2,000 and leaves 30 million homeless.

1998

In October, Hurricane Mitch strikes Central America, killing about 11,000 and leaving 1.5 million homeless.

1999

On May 3, a tornado outbreak occurs in Oklahoma. More than 50 tornadoes tear across the state in one day, killing more than 40 people.

Tornado, US Midwest

1999

An earthquake along Turkey's North Anatolian Fault destroys 150,000 buildings in Izmit, killing 17,000 people.

2001

In January, an earthquake in Gujarat, India, flattens 400,000 buildings, many of them poorly constructed, killing 20,000 people.

2001

On January 31, massive mudslides caused by an earthquake in El Salvador kill 265 people in the capital, San Salvador.

Health workers, SARS outbreak, 2002

2002

Severe Acute Respiratory Syndrome (SARS), a previously unknown viral disease, first appears in Guandong, China.

2003

On December 27, an earthquake destroys the ancient city of Bam, Iran, killing 26,000.

2004

On December 26, a tsunami in the Indian Ocean kills over 300,000 people.

2005

In August, the category 5 Hurricane Katrina hits the southern US.

2005

On October 8, over 86,000 people are killed by a magnitude 7.6 earthquake in northern Pakistan and parts of Kashmir.

Find out more

Although you probably would not want to be around when a natural disaster is happening, you can find out more about natural disasters by visiting some of the places mentioned in this book. You could investigate flood defenses at London's Thames Barrier, visit the volcanic geysers in Yellowstone Park, in Montana and Wyoming, or take a trip back in time in Pompeii, Italy. There is lots more information about natural disasters on the Internet, too, including up-to-date news of the latest events.

PLACES TO VISIT

Many large cities have museums that have in-depth exhibits about Earth's structure, the weather, and space. Check your local telephone directory, visit the library, or search the Internet to find out about natural history museums in your area.

Smithsonian Institution
Washington, DC
(202) 633-1000
www.si.edu

American Museum of Natural History
New York, NY
(212) 769-5100
www.amnh.org

Field Museum
Chicago, IL
(312) 922-9410
www.fieldmuseum.org

California Academy of Sciences
San Francisco, CA
(415) 321-8000
www.calacademy.org

YELLOWSTONE
The world's first national park owes its creation to its spectacular geological features. Its geysers, bubbling mud, and hot springs are signs of a huge underground magma chamber.

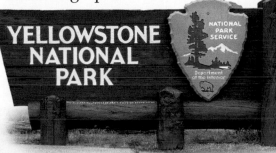

Yellowstone National Park, founded in 1872

RICHTER SCALE

1	2	3	4	5	6	7	8	9

Recorded on local seismographs, but not generally felt by people — Felt by most; causes little damage — Felt widely; slight damage near epicenter — Large earthquake causes damage to poorly constructed buildings within dozens of miles — Major earthquake causes damage in an area up to 60 miles (100 km) across epicenter — Great earthquake causes destruction and loss of life across several hundred miles — Rare great earthquake causes major damage over 600 miles (1,000 km)

Information websites classify earthquakes using the Richter scale. The seismic waves recorded for a magnitude 4 earthquake have an amplitude (height) ten times greater than those produced by a magnitude 3 earthquake.

Radar truck used by storm trackers

USEFUL WEBSITES

- **www.tsunami.org** for the Pacific Tsunami Museum
- **www.volcano.und.nodak.edu** for information about volcanoes
- **weather.noaa.gov** for the US National Weather Service
- **weather.yahoo.com** for weather forecasts anywhere in the world and information about severe weather
- **www.panda.org**, then click on "climate change" to see the Worldwide Fund for Nature's information about climate change

- **www.fema.gov** (in the United States) or **www.psepc.gc.ca** (in Canada) to find out about environmental dangers, such as potential floods, that exist in your area, and how to prepare for them
- **www.stormtrack.org** for information about people who track tornadoes
- **www.epa.gov/globalwarming/kids** to find out about global warming
- **www.who.int** to find out about world health risks from the World Health Organization

SAFFIR-SIMPSON SCALE
The Saffir-Simpson scale classifies hurricanes according to the intensity of sustained wind speeds. Short gusts may reach even faster speeds, during the storm. Less than one percent of all hurricanes are classified category 5.

Category	1	2	3	4	5
Description	Weak	Moderate	Strong	Very strong	Devastating
Wind, mph (km/h)	75–95 (120–153)	96–110 (154–177)	111–130 (178–209)	131–155 (210–249)	156+ (250+)
Storm surge, ft (m)	4–5 (1.2–1.5)	6–8 (1.6–2.4)	9–12 (2.5–3.7)	13–18 (3.8–5.5)	18+ (5.5+)
Damage	Minimal. Some tree damage	Moderate. Major damage to mobile homes; roofs damaged	Extensive. Mobile homes destroyed; large trees blown down	Extreme. Roofs of small buildings destroyed; windows blown in	Catastrophic. Roofs of many larger buildings destroyed

Glossary

ACID RAIN Rain made more acidic by air pollution from vehicle exhausts and emissions from factories.

AFTERSHOCK A smaller earth tremor that comes after the main shock of an earthquake. These aftershocks may continue for months.

AIR MASS A body of air with a fairly uniform temperature that may stretch over thousands of miles within the troposphere.

ATMOSPHERE The layer of gases that surrounds Earth.

AVALANCHE A large mass of snow sliding down a mountainside.

BACTERIA (singular bacterium) Microscopic single-celled organisms that lack a nucleus. Some can cause disease.

BORE A giant wave, created by an exceptionally high tide, that rushes up low-lying rivers.

BUOY A float anchored in water, usually to mark a position. Ocean-monitoring devices can be attached to buoys that can transmit information to satellites.

CARBON A nonmetallic element that occurs in the form of graphite, diamond and charcoal, and forms many compounds.

CLIMATE The regular pattern of weather in a particular region.

CRATER A bowl-shaped depression at the mouth of a volcano or caused by the impact of a meteorite.

CRUST Earth's thin, rocky outer layer.

CUMULONIMBUS CLOUD A towering white or gray cloud that may bring thunderstorms or hail.

DROUGHT A long period with little or no rainfall.

DUST DEVIL A small twisting wind that lifts dust and debris into the air.

EARTHQUAKE A series of vibrations in Earth's crust, caused by movement at a fault in or between tectonic plates.

EL NIÑO A change in atmospheric and ocean conditions that causes warm water currents in the Pacific Ocean to flow east instead of west. El Niño occurs every few years and can disrupt the weather around the world.

EMBANKMENT A bank of soil or stone, often used to protect an area from flooding.

ENVIRONMENT The conditions and surroundings in which something exists.

EPICENTER The point on Earth's surface directly above the focus of an earthquake.

EPIDEMIC An outbreak of a contagious disease that spreads rapidly.

ERUPTION An outpouring of hot gases, lava, and other material from a volcano.

EVACUATION An organized departure of residents from an area threatened by disaster.

Crater of Mount Vesuvius, Italy

FAULT A fracture in Earth's crust along which rocks have moved relative to one another. Transform faults occur where two tectonic plates slide past one another.

FLASH FLOOD A flood that occurs suddenly after heavy rain.

FLOOD An overflow of water onto ground that is normally dry.

FLOOD DEFENSES Structures such as dams, embankments, levees, and sluices, which are designed to redirect floodwaters in order to protect land from flooding.

FLOOD PLAIN The area of flat land around a river where the river naturally floods.

FOCUS A point within Earth's crust where an earthquake originates.

Aialik Glacier, Alaska

FOSSIL FUEL A fuel such as coal or oil that is derived from the remains of once-living organisms buried beneath the ground.

FRONT The forward-moving edge of an air mass. A cold front is the leading edge of a cold air mass, and a warm front is the leading edge of a warm air mass.

GLACIER A mass of year-round ice and snow that is capable of flowing slowly downhill. The largest glaciers are the Antarctic and Greenland ice sheets.

GLOBAL WARMING A gradual increase in average temperature worldwide.

GROUNDWATER Water that collects in, or flows through, rocks beneath Earth's surface.

HABITAT The natural home of a living organism.

HAILSTONE A hard pellet of ice that falls from a cumulonimbus thundercloud during a hailstorm.

HOT SPOT A site of volcanic activity far from the edges of the tectonic plates caused by magma rising from the mantle.

Lava flowing on Mount Etna

HURRICANE A violent storm bringing powerful twisting winds and torrential rain. Hurricanes are known as cyclones in the Indian Ocean and typhoons in the Pacific Ocean.

ICE AGE A period of time when ice sheets cover a large part of Earth's surface.

IRRIGATION A system for supplying farmland with water by means of channels.

LANDSLIDE A large mass or rock or soil that slides down a hillside or breaks away from a cliff.

LAVA Molten rock that erupts from a volcano. When this material is underground, it is called magma.

LEVEE A natural or artificial embankment that prevents a river from overflowing.

LIGHTNING The visible flash that occurs during a thunderstorm when electricity is discharged between a cloud and the ground or between two clouds.

Rickshaw drivers ride through monsoon floods in Guwahati, India

MAGMA Molten rock beneath Earth's surface. Above the ground, it is called lava.

METEORITE A piece of solid material that travels from space, through Earth's atmosphere, to land on Earth.

METEOROLOGIST A scientist who studies the weather.

MOLTEN Melted to form a hot liquid.

MONSOON A seasonal wind which, when it blows from the southwest, brings heavy summer rains to southern Asia.

OZONE LAYER The layer of gas in the stratosphere that helps protect Earth from the Sun's harmful radiation.

PANDEMIC An outbreak of disease that spreads to a vast number of people over a wide area.

PYROCLASTIC FLOW An fast-flowing and destructive outpouring of hot ash, rock and gases from a volcano.

RADAR A system for detecting distant objects by means of reflected radio waves, in order to determine their size, position, and movement. Radar can be used to detect a developing tornado inside a storm cloud.

RICHTER SCALE A scale used for measuring the intensity of earthquakes, with 9+ indicating the strongest tremors.

SAFFIR-SIMPSON SCALE A scale used to measure the intensity of hurricanes. Category 5 indicates the most severe hurricanes.

SATELLITE An object that orbits a planet. Artificial satellites in orbit around Earth are used to monitor the weather, ground movements, and changes in sea level.

SEISMIC Caused by an earthquake.

SEISMOGRAM A record of seismic activity on paper or computer produced by a seismograph.

SEISMOGRAPH A device for detecting, recording, and measuring earth tremors.

SLUICE A human-made channel with a gate for regulating water flow, used to redirect excess water in order to prevent flooding.

SMOG Fog polluted with smoke.

SONAR A system for detecting underwater objects and surfaces by means of reflected sound waves.

Supercell cloud

STORM SURGE An unusually high tide produced by the low-pressure eye of a hurricane.

STRATOSPHERE The layer of Earth's atmosphere above the troposphere where the ozone layer is found.

SUNSPOT A dark area that appears on the surface of the Sun where magnetic forces hold the light back.

SUPERCELL CLOUD A huge storm cloud that may produce a tornado.

TECTONIC PLATE One of about 20 pieces that make up Earth's crust. The parts of the plates that carry the continents are denser and thicker than the parts beneath the oceans.

THUNDER The sound of air expanding rapidly when it is heated by lightning.

TORNADO A spinning wind that appears as a dark, funnel-shaped cloud reaching down to the ground.

TREMOR A shaking or vibrating movement.

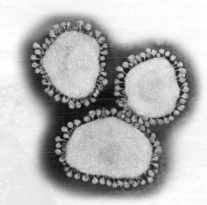

Coronavirus particles

TROPOSPHERE The layer of the atmosphere closest to Earth's surface where all weather happens.

TSUNAMI A fast-moving ocean wave, or series of waves, generated by tectonic movements or by an object impacting the water surface.

VENT An opening in a volcano through which lava or volcanic gases flow.

VIRUS An infectious agent comprising a microscopic package of chemicals surrounded by a protein coat. Viruses invade living cells and usually destroy them in order to reproduce.

VOLCANO An opening in the crust of Earth through which lava escapes.

VOLCANOLOGIST A scientist who studies volcanoes.

VORTEX A tightly spiraling mass of liquid or gas.

WATERSPOUT A tornado that occurs over water, producing a column of spinning mist and spray.

WAVE CREST The highest point of a wave.

WAVE TROUGH The lowest point of a wave.

Index

Acknowledgments

The publisher would like to thank the following for their kind permission to reproduce their photographs:

Abbreviations key: t=top, b=bottom, r=right, l=left, c=center, a=above

1 Science Photo Library: NOAA. 2 Corbis: Jim Reed (br); Roger Ressmeyer (tr). 2 Getty Images: Jimin Lai/AFP (br). 2 Rex Features: HXL (tl). 3 DK Images: Courtesy of Glasgow Museum (tr); Courtesy of the Museo Archeologico Nazionale di Napoli (bl). Photolibrary.com: Warren Faidley/OSF (tl). Science Photo Library: Planetary Visions Ltd (cr); Zephyr (br). 4 www.bridgeman.co.uk: The Great Wave of Kanagawa, from 'Thirty six views of Mount Fuji', c.1831, colour woodblock print (detail) by Hokusai, Katsushika, Tokyo Fuji Art Museum, Tokyo, Japan (bl). Corbis: Dan Lamont (br). DK Images: (tl); Michael Zabe CONACULTA-INAH-MEX. Authorized reproduction by the Instituto Nacional de Antropologia. Rex Features: Masatoshi Okauchi (cr), Science Photo Library: NASA (tr). 5 Corbis: Alfio Scigliano/Sygma. 6 Corbis: Noboru Hashimoto (b). Getty Images: Jim Sugar/Science Faction (c). Science Photo Library: (tr); Planetary Visions Ltd (tl). 7 Corbis: Frans Lanting (tr). Getty Images: Aaron McCoy/Lonely Planet Images (cl); Andres Hernandez/Getty Images News (b). Science Photo Library: Eye of Science (cr). 8 DK Images: Courtesy of the Natural History Museum, London (t). 9 Corbis: (cl); Kevin Schafer (cr). Rob Francis: (b). 10 www.bridgeman.co.uk: The Great Wave of Kanagawa, from 'Thirty six views of Mount Fuji', c.1831, colour woodblock print (detail) by Hokusai, Katsushika, Tokyo Fuji Art Museum, Tokyo, Japan (br). Corbis: Academy of Natural Sciences of Philadelphia (tr); Reuters (br). Science Photo Library: Stephen & Donna O'Meara (cl). 11 Science Photo Library: Digital Globe, Eurimage (tl). 12 Corbis: Lloyd Cluff (b). Science Photo Library: George Bernard (c). 12–13 Tony Friedkin/Sony Pictures Classics/ZUMA. 13 Corbis: (cr). Empics Ltd: AP (tl). Associate Professor Ted Bryant, Associate Dean of Science, University of Wollongong (t). 14 Corbis: Dadang

Tri/Reuters (tl). Empics Ltd: AP (br). Rex Features: SIPA (b). 15 Empics Ltd: (cr); Karim Khamzin/AP (b). Panos Pictures: Tim A. Hetherington (cl). Reuters: Amateur Video Grab (t). 16 Corbis: Thomas Thompson/WFP/Handout/Reuters (cl). Getty Images: Jimin Lai/AFP (b). 16–17 Corbis: Dieter Telemans. 16–17 Corbis: Babu/Reuters (c). 17 Corbis: Bazuki Muhammas/Reuters (bl); Yuriko Nakao (tl). Rex Features: RSR (br). 18 Empics Ltd: Wang Xiaochuan/AP (tr). Rex Features: HXL (tl); Nick Cornish (NCH) (t); SS/Keystone USA (KUS) (cl). 18–19 Corbis: Chaiwat Subprasom/Reuters (b). 19 Rex Features: IJO (br); Roy Garner (c). 20 Getty Images: Getty Images News (b). Panos Pictures: Dean Chapman (tl). Rex Features: Masatoshi Okauchi (tr). 21 Corbis: Chaiwat Subprasom/Reuters (r). Empics Ltd: Lucy Pemoni/AP (tr). Getty Images: Getty Images News (cl). Science Photo Library: David Ducros (tl); US Geological Survey (bl). 22 Corbis: Reuters (br). Science Photo Library: Georg Gerster (cl). 23 Corbis: Owen Franken (cr). DK Images: Science Museum, London (cr). Science Photo Library: NASA (bl); Zephyr (br). 24 Corbis: Kurt Stier (cl); Patrick Robert/Sygma (tr); Ryan Pyle (b). 24–25 Rex Features: Sipa Press (b). 25 Corbis: Andrea Comas/Reuters (br); Michael S. Yamashita (tr). 26 Corbis: Jose Fuste Raga (br). © Michael Holford: (tl). FLPA – Images of Nature: S.Jonasson (bl). 26–27 Science Photo Library: Bernhard Edmaier (b). 27 Corbis: Reuters (cr). Science Photo Library: Mauro Fermariello (cl). 28 Corbis: Gary Braasch (tl); Roger Ressmeyer (cl). 28–29 Corbis: Alfio Scigliano/Sygma (bc). 29 www.bridgeman. co.uk: Private Collection, Archives Charmet (cl). Corbis: Alberto Garcia (r). DK Images: Courtesy of the Museo Archeologico Nazionale di Napoli (br). Empics Ltd: Itsuo Inouye/AP Photo (cr). 30 Corbis: John Van Hasselt (tr); Lowell Georgia (tr); S.P. Gillette (cl). Getty Images: Vedros & Associates/The Image Bank (bl). Science Photo Library: Mark Clarke (br). 31 Corbis: Jonathan Blair (tr); Reuters (bl), (bc). Robert Harding Picture Library: Tony Waltham (b). 32 Alamy Images: Andrew Parker (br). 32–33 Science Photo Library: NASA (t). 33 Corbis: Christopher Morris (bl). US Marine Corps: Gunnery Sgt. Shannon Arledge (br). 34 Science

Photo Library: Jean-Loup Charmet (tl). 34–35 Science Photo Library: Kent Wood (c). 35 Corbis: George Hall (t). FLPA – Images of Nature: Jim Reed (br). Science Photo Library: Jim Reed (cb); Peter Menzel (t). 36 Science Photo Library: Colin Cuthbert (tr); NOAA (b). 37 Photolibrary.com: Warren Faidley/OSF (b); Warren Faidley/OSF (tr). Science Photo Library: Jim Reed (c); NOAA (tl). 38 Corbis: Reuters (b). Science Photo Library: Chris Sattlberger (tl). 38–39 Science Photo Library: NASA/Goddard Space Flight Center (t). 39 Empics Ltd: Dave Martin/AP (br). Getty Images: Ed Pritchard/Stone (c). FLPA – Images of Nature: (tr). 40 Corbis: Irwin Thompson/Dallas Morning News (bl); Smiley N. Pool/Dallas Morning News (cl); Vincent Laforet/Pool/Reuters (br). 41 Corbis: Irwin Thompson/Dallas Morning News (t); Ken Cedeno (c); Michael Ainsworth/Dallas Morning News (br). 41–41 Science Photo Library: NOAA (c). 42 Photolibrary.com: Warren Faidley/OSF (c), (bl), (bc), (br). 43 Photolibrary. com: Warren Faidley/OSF (cl). Corbis: Science Photo Library: J.G. Golden (cr); Jim Reed (bl); Mary Beth Angelo (tr). 44 Getty Images: AFP (tr). 44–45 Corbis: Reuters (bc). 45 Corbis: Jim Reed (bc); Reuters (tr); Tom Bean (tr). 46 DK Images: Michael Zabe CONACULTA-INAH-MEX. Authorized reproduction by the Instituto Nacional de Antropologia. 46–47 Corbis: Reuters (b). 47 Corbis: Brooks Kraft (tr); Rafiqur Rahman/Reuters (br); Romeo Ranoco/Reuters (c). Magnum: Philip Jones-Griffiths (cr). 48 Corbis: Despotovic Dusko/Sygma (cl). Magnum: Steve McCurry (bl). Science Photo Library: Novosti Photo Library (r). 48–49 Corbis: Reuters (cb). 49 Corbis: Howard Davies (br). Getty Images: Time Life Pictures (b). Photolibrary.com: Sarah Puttnam/Index Stock Imagery (tr). 50 Corbis: Polypix, Eye Ubiquitous (tl); Stephenie Maze (bl). FLPA– Images of Nature: Ben Van den Brink/Foto Natura (cl). Science Photo Library: NASA (tr). 50–51 Corbis: Jonathan Blair. 51 Corbis: Douglas Faulkner (tl); Ed Kashi (tr). 52 NASA: (cl). Panos Pictures: Paul Lowe (c). 52–53 Corbis: Steven K. Doi/ZUMA. 53 Corbis: Dan Lamont (t). Panos Pictures: Dean Sewell (c). 54 Science Photo Library: (t); NASA (cl), (cr). 54–55 Corbis: Hans Strand. 55 Science Photo Library:

Alexis Rosenfield (cl); British Antarctic Survey (cr). 56 Science Photo Library: BSIG, M.I.G./BAEZA (bl); David Hay Jones (tl); NASA. 56–57 Getty Images: Steven Wienberg/Photographer's Choice. 57 FLPA – Images of Nature: Norbert Wu/Minden Pictures (cr). Magnum: Jean Gaumy (tl). Science Photo Library: Simon Fraser (br). Still Pictures: W. Ming (tr). 58 Empics Ltd: David Guttenfelder/AP (bl); Jordan Peter/PA (tl). Science Photo Library: John Burbridge tr. 58–59 Science Photo Library: Colin Cuthbert. 59 Science Photo Library: Andrew Syred (tr); Astrid & Hanns-Frieder Michler (tl); Eye of Science (cr). 60 Empics Ltd: John Moore/AP (bl). Eye Ubiquitous: Hutchison (br). Science Photo Library: James King-Holmes (tl). 61 Corbis: Erik de Castro/Reuters (br); Pallava Bagla (t). Science Photo Library: AJ Photo/Hop American (cr); Andy Crump, TDR, WHO (tr); CDC (cl); NIBSC (bc); Jeff Vanuga (tr); Roger Ressmeyer (bl). 62 Corbis: Claro Cortes IV/Reuters (bc); Roger Ressmeyer (bl). Science Photo Library: CDC/C. Goldsmith/J. Katz/S. Zaki (cr). 63 Corbis: Roger Ressmeyer (tr). Science Photo Library: NASA (tl), (b). 64 Corbis: Reuters (br); Sally A. Morgan, Ecoscene (l); Ted Soqui (tr). 64–65 Science Photo Library: NASA, background. 65 Corbis: Reuters (l); Vinve Streano (br). Science Photo Library: Russell Kightley (tr). 66 Corbis: Gianni Dagli Orti (bl). The Art Archive: (tr). 66 Science Photo Library: Mehau Kulyk (tl); Photo Researchers (tr). 66–67 Rob Francis: background. 66–67 Getty Images: Fraser Hall/Robert Harding World Imagery (bc). 67 Photolibrary.com: Mary Plage/OSF (cra). Corbis: Bettmann (br). Science Photo Library: Bettmann (tc). 68 Corbis: Faisal Mahmood/Reuters (bl); Reuters (cr). Science Photo Library: Eric Nguyen/Jim Reed Photography (tr). 68–69 Rob Francis: background. 69 Corbis: Reuters (bl). 70 Science Photo Library: Jeremy Bishop (cr). 71 Corbis: Reuters (t). Science Photo Library: Dr Linda Stannard, UCT (cr); Jim Reed (bc).

All other images © Dorling Kindersley.
For further information see: www.dkimages.com